W9-DEC-729

ILLUSTRATED PSALMS
OF THE
JERUSALEM BIBLE

ILLUSTRATED
PSALMS
OF THE
JERUSALEM
BIBLE

Alexander Jones, General Editor
Fannie Drossos, Illustrator

1977

DOUBLEDAY & COMPANY, INC.
GARDEN CITY, NEW YORK

The abridged introductions and notes of this volume of The Psalms are based on those which appear in *La Bible de Jérusalem* (one-volume edition) published by Les Editions du Cerf, Paris. The English text, though translated from the ancient texts, owes a large debt to the work of the many scholars who collaborated to produce *La Bible de Jérusalem,* which the publishers of this volume gratefully acknowledge.

FIRST EDITION

Library of Congress Cataloging in Publication Data

Bible. O.T. Psalms. English. Jerusalem Bible. 1977.
Illustrated Psalms of the Jerusalem Bible.

I. Jones, Alexander, 1906–   II. Drossos, Fannie.
III. Title.
BS1422 1977   223'.2'052
ISBN: 0-385-12286-1
Library of Congress Catalog Card Number 76–23769

Introduction

THE PSALTER, or Book of Psalms, is a collection of hymns used in the liturgical worship of the Temple; it is arranged in five "books" or parts. Some of the psalms can be identified as written for one or other of the great festivals (for example the group called "Songs of Ascents," which are for the annual pilgrimage); others cannot be so simply defined, and it may well be that the liturgical use of them changed during the eventful years of Israel's history.

The 150 psalms* represent the work of several centuries. There are some which can be dated from the Exile and some after the return to Jerusalem, and others which are clearly allied to the wisdom writings of later times; but there are also psalms which belong to the period of the kings and among these there may be psalms as early as David himself, traditionally the writer and singer of songs. Although the inscriptions appear to ascribe many of the psalms to David, it should be noted that these inscriptions actually refer to different collections of the hymns made at different times or places; it is the existence of these separate collections which explains the duplication of a few psalms in the Psalter. Nevertheless, an early editor accepted some of the inscriptions as indications of authorship, and added annotations on the probable occasion of their writing.

The psalms have for so long been used in Christian worship that their early origins are often overlooked; like all lyrical poetry, they express passion—and in their own time there was nothing improper about violent curses against enemies and oppressors or against the unfaithful, nor about a frank longing for revenge and massacre. These are notes which can be found in the psalms and, like the name Yahweh, must be accepted as a part of the world of the psalmists. But the principal kinds of psalms which can be distinguished by their subjects include: hymns of praise, often recalling the mighty works of God in the past history of the nation; prayers of entreaty or penitence, either personal or collective; thanksgivings; wisdom psalms and praise of the Law; prophetic oracles; royal psalms. The royal psalms are addressed to kings, the successors of David, and often include prophecies of their future glory; after the end of the monarchy, these oracles together with the prophecies of the renewal of Zion became a focus of the messianic hope, and they are commonly accepted as such by the writers of the New Testament.

---

* From Ps. 10 to Ps. 148 the numbering of the Hebrew Bible (adopted here) is one figure ahead of the Greek and the Vulgate, which join 9 and 10 and also 114 and 115, but divide both 116 and 147 into two.

ILLUSTRATED PSALMS
OF THE
JERUSALEM BIBLE

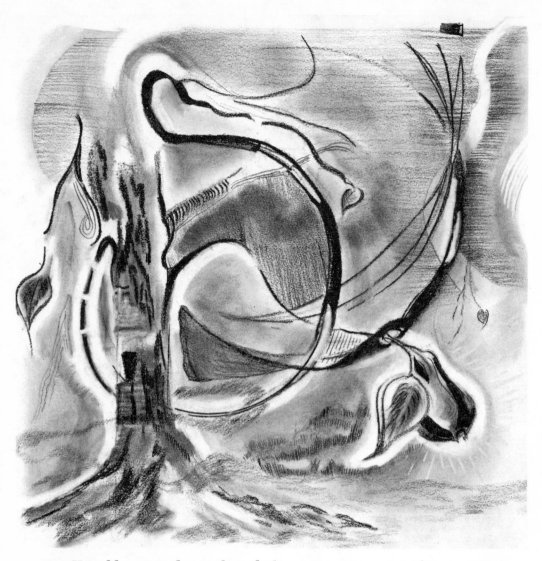

He is like a tree that is planted / by water streams, / yielding its fruit in season, / its leaves never fading; / success attends all he does. / It is nothing like this with the wicked, nothing like this!
(*Psalm 1:3–4*)

Psalm 1

THE TWO WAYS

[1] Happy the man
  who never follows the advice of the wicked,
  or loiters on the way that sinners take,
  or sits about with scoffers,
[2] but finds his pleasure in the law of Yahweh,
  and murmurs his law day and night.

[3] He is like a tree that is planted
  by water streams,
  yielding its fruit in season,
  its leaves never fading;
  success attends all he does.
[4] It is nothing like this with the wicked, nothing like this!

  No, these are like chaff
  blown away by the wind.
[5] The wicked will not stand firm when Judgment comes,
  nor sinners when the virtuous assemble.
[6] For Yahweh takes care of the way the virtuous go,
  but the way of the wicked is doomed.

"Now let us break their fetters! / Now let us throw off their yoke!"
(*Psalm 2:3*)

Psalm 2

[1] Why this uproar among the nations?
 Why this impotent muttering of pagans—
[2] kings on earth rising in revolt,
 princes plotting against Yahweh and his Anointed,
[3] "Now let us break their fetters!
 Now let us throw off their yoke!"

[4] The One whose throne is in heaven sits laughing,
 Yahweh derides them.
[5] Then angrily he addresses them,
 in a rage he strikes them with panic,
[6] "This is my king, installed by me
 on Zion, my holy mountain."

[7] Let me proclaim Yahweh's decree;
 he has told me, "You are my son,
 today I have become your father.
[8] Ask and I will give you the nations for your heritage,
 the ends of the earth for your domain.
[9] With iron scepter you will break them,
 shatter them like potter's ware."

[10] So now, you kings, learn wisdom,
 earthly rulers, be warned:
[11] serve Yahweh, fear him,
[12] tremble and kiss his feet,
 or he will be angry and you will perish,
 for his anger is very quick to blaze.

Happy all who take shelter in him.

Loudly I cry to Yahweh, / and he answers me from his holy mountain.
(*Psalm 3:4*)

Psalm 3

Psalm Of David When he was escaping from his son Absalom

MORNING PRAYER OF THE VIRTUOUS MAN
UNDER PERSECUTION

[1] Yahweh, more and more are turning against me,
more and more rebelling against me,
[2] more and more saying about me,
"There is no help for him in his God." *Pause*
[3] But, Yahweh, my encircling shield,
my glory, you help me hold up my head.
[4] Loudly I cry to Yahweh,
and he answers me from his holy mountain. *Pause*

[5] Now I can lie down and go to sleep
and then awake, for Yahweh has hold of me:
[6] no fear now of those tens of thousands
posted against me wherever I turn. *Pause*

[7]   Rise, Yahweh!
   Save me, my God!
You hack all my enemies to the cheekbone,
you break the teeth of the wicked.
[8]   From Yahweh, rescue.
   On your people, blessing!

God, guardian of my rights, you answer when I call, / when I am in trouble, you come to my relief; / now be good to me and hear my prayer.
(Psalm 4:1)

Psalm 4

For the choirmaster For strings Psalm Of David

EVENING PRAYER

[1] God, guardian of my rights, you answer when I call,
    when I am in trouble, you come to my relief;
    now be good to me and hear my prayer.

[2] You men, why shut your hearts so long,
  loving delusions, chasing after lies? *Pause*

[3] Know this, Yahweh works wonders for those he loves,
  Yahweh hears me when I call to him.
[4]   Tremble: give up sinning,
spend your night in quiet meditation. *Pause*
[5] Offer sacrifice in a right spirit, and trust Yahweh.

[6] "Who will give us sight of happiness?" many say.
  Show us the light of your face, turned toward us!

[7] Yahweh, ·you have given more joy to my heart
  than others ever knew, for all their corn and wine.

[8] In peace I lie down, and fall asleep at once,
  since you alone, Yahweh, make me rest secure.

Psalm 5

For the choirmaster   For flutes   Psalm   Of David

MORNING PRAYER

¹ Yahweh, let my words come to your ears,
    spare a thought for my sighs.
² Listen to my cry for help,
    my King and my God!

³ I say this prayer to you, ·Yahweh,
    for at daybreak you listen for my voice;
and at dawn I hold myself in readiness for you,
    I watch for you.

⁴ You are not a God who is pleased with wickedness,
    you have no room for the wicked;
⁵ boasters collapse
    under your scrutiny.

You hate all evil men,
⁶   liars you destroy;
murderers and frauds
    Yahweh detests.

⁷ But I, so great is your love,
    may come to your house,
and before your holy Temple bow down
    in reverence to you.

⁸ Yahweh, lead me in the path of your righteousness,
    for there are men lying in wait for me;
make your way plain before me.

⁹ Not a word from their lips can be trusted,
    deep within them lies ruin,
their throats are yawning graves;
    they make their tongues so smooth!

¹⁰ Pronounce them guilty, God,
    make their intrigues their own downfall!
Hound them for their countless crimes,
    since they have rebelled against you.

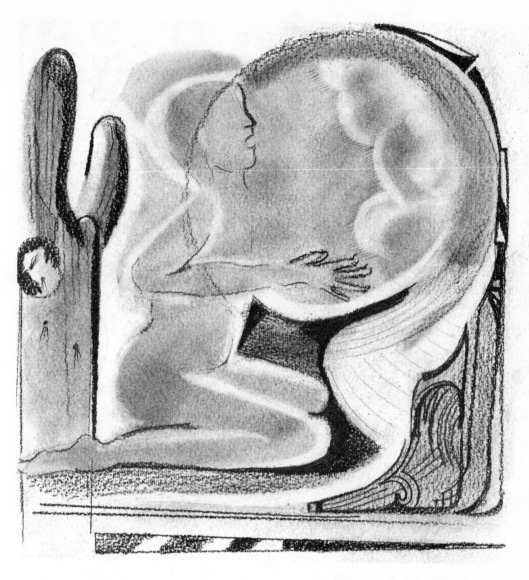

Yahweh, let my words come to your ears, / spare a thought for my sighs.
(*Psalm 5:1*)

[11] But joy for all who take shelter in you,
    endless shouts of joy!
Since you protect them, they exult in you,
    those who love your name.

[12] It is you who bless the virtuous man, Yahweh;
    your favor is like a shield covering him.

Yahweh, do not punish me in your rage, / or reprove me in the heat of anger.
(Psalm 6:1)

Psalm 6

For the choirmaster   For strings, for the octachord   Psalm   Of David

PRAYER IN ORDEAL

[1] Yahweh, do not punish me in your rage,
  or reprove me in the heat of anger.
[2] Pity me, Yahweh, I have no strength left,
  heal me, my bones are in torment,
[3] my soul is in utter torment.
  Yahweh, how long will you be?

[4] Come back, Yahweh, rescue my soul,
  save me, if you love me;
[5] for in death there is no remembrance of you:
  who can sing your praises in Sheol?

[6] I am worn out with groaning,
  every night I drench my pillow
  and soak my bed with tears;
[7] my eye is wasted with grief,
  I have grown old with enemies all around me.

[8] Away from me, all you evil men!
  For Yahweh has heard the sound of my weeping;
[9] Yahweh has heard my petition,
  Yahweh will accept my prayer.
[10] Let all my enemies, discredited, in utter torment,
  fall back in sudden confusion.

Psalm 7

Lamentation Of David, who sang it to Yahweh about Cush the Benjaminite

PRAYER OF THE VIRTUOUS UNDER PERSECUTION

¹ Yahweh my God, I take shelter in you;
  from all who hound me, save me, rescue me,
² or, like a lion he will carry me off
  and tear me to pieces where no one can save me.

³ Yahweh my God, if I ever
  soiled my hands with fraud,
⁴ repaid a friend evil for good,
  spared a man who wronged me,
⁵ then let the enemy hound me down and catch me,
  let him stamp my life into the ground,
  and leave my entrails lying in the dust!   *Pause*

⁶ Rise, Yahweh, in anger,
    awake, my God!
  Confront the raging of my enemies,
    you who demand that justice shall be done.
⁷ Let the nations muster around you in a body,
    and then return, high over them.
⁸ (Yahweh is arbiter of nations.)

  Give judgment for me, Yahweh: as my virtue
    and my integrity deserve.
⁹ Bring the maliciousness of evil men to an end,
    set the virtuous on his feet,
    you righteous God,
  assessor of mind and heart.

¹⁰ God is the shield that protects me,
    he preserves upright hearts,
¹¹ God the righteous judge
    is slow to show his anger,
  but he is a God who is always enraged
¹²   by those who refuse to repent.

  The enemy may sharpen his sword,
  he may bend his bow and take aim,
¹³ but the weapons he prepares will kill himself
  and his arrows turn into firebrands.

Rise, Yahweh, in anger, / awake, my god! / Confront the raging of my enemies, / you who demand that justice shall be done.
(Psalm 7:6)

[14] Look at him, pregnant with wickedness,
   conceiving Spite, he gives birth to Mishap.
[15] He dug a pit, hollowed it out,
   only to fall into his own trap!
[16] His spite recoils on his own head,
   his brutality falls back on his own skull.

[17] I give thanks to Yahweh for his righteousness,
   I sing praise to the name of the Most High.

birds in the air, fish in the sea / traveling the paths of the ocean.
(Psalm 8:8)

Psalm 8

For the choirmaster   On the . . . of Gath   Psalm   Of David

THE MUNIFICENCE OF THE CREATOR

1 Yahweh, our Lord,
  how great your name throughout the earth!

Above the heavens is your majesty chanted
2 by the mouths of children, babes in arms.
  You set your stronghold firm against your foes
  to subdue enemies and rebels.

3 I look up at your heavens, made by your fingers,
  at the moon and stars you set in place—
4 ah, what is man that you should spare a thought for him,
  the son of man that you should care for him?

5 Yet you have made him little less than a god,
  you have crowned him with glory and splendor,
6 made him lord over the work of your hands,
  set all things under his feet,

7 sheep and oxen, all these,
  yes, wild animals too,
8 birds in the air, fish in the sea
  traveling the paths of the ocean.

9 Yahweh, our Lord,
  how great your name throughout the earth!

Psalm 9–10

For the choirmaster For oboe and harp Psalm Of David

GOD CRUSHES THE WICKED AND SAVES THE HUMBLE

[1] I thank you, Yahweh, with all my heart;
  I recite your marvels one by one,
[2] I rejoice and exult in you,
  I sing praise to your name, Most High.

[3] My enemies are in retreat,
  stumbling, perishing as you confront them:
[4] you have upheld the justice of my cause
  from the throne where you sit as righteous judge.

[5] You have checked the nations, you have crushed the wicked,
  blotted out their name for ever and ever;
[6] the enemy is finished, in everlasting ruin,
  you have overthrown cities, their memory has perished.

[7] See, ·Yahweh is enthroned for ever,
  he sets up his throne for judgment;
[8] he is going to judge the world with justice,
  and pronounce a true verdict on the nations.

[9] May Yahweh be a stronghold for the oppressed,
  a stronghold when times are hard.
[10] Those who acknowledge your name can rely on you,
  you never desert those who seek you, Yahweh.

[11] To Yahweh with his home in Zion, sing praise,
  tell the nations of his mighty actions;
[12] he, the avenger of blood, remembers them,
  he does not ignore the cry of the wretched.

[13] Take pity on me, Yahweh, look on my suffering,
  you who lift me back from the gates of death,
[14] that in the gates of the daughter of Zion
  I may recite your praises one by one, rejoicing that you have saved me.

[15] The nations have sunk into a pit of their own making,
  they are caught by the feet in the snare they set themselves.
[16] Yahweh has made himself known, has given judgment,
  he has trapped the wicked in the work of their own hands. *Muted music*

[17] May the wicked return to Sheol, *Pause*

My enemies are in retreat, / stumbling, perishing as you confront them:
(*Psalm 9:3*)

    all the nations forgetful of God.
[18] For the needy is not always forgotten,
    the hope of the poor is never brought to nothing.

[19] Rise, Yahweh, let not man have the upper hand,
    let the nations stand trial before you!
[20] Strike terror into them, Yahweh,
    let the nations know they are only men! *Pause*

10

1 Yahweh, why do you stand aside,
  why hide from us now the times are hard?
2 The poor man is devoured by the pride of the wicked,
  he is caught in the wiles that the other has devised.

3 The evil man boasts of his soul's desires,
  the grasping man blasphemes, the wicked spurns Yahweh.
4 "His anger is up there, he will not make me pay!
  There is no God!" This is the way his mind works.

5 At every moment his course is assured,
  your rulings are too lofty for his notice;
  his rivals? He sneers at them all.

6 "Nothing can shake me," he assures himself.
7 Himself untouched by disaster, ·he curses others.

  Fraud and oppression fill his mouth,
  spite and iniquity are under his tongue;
8 there in the reeds he lies in ambush
  to kill the innocent where no one can see.

  Peering and prying for the out of luck,
9 lurking unseen like a lion in his hide,
  lurking to capture the poor man,
  the poor man seized, he drags him away in his net.

10 Questing of eye, he stoops, he crouches,
  and the luckless wretch falls into his power
11 as he thinks to himself, "God forgets,
  he hides his face, he does not see at all."

12 Rise, Yahweh, God raise your hand,
  do not forget the poor!
13 Why does the wicked man spurn God,
  assuring himself, "He will not make me pay?"

14 You yourself have seen the distress and the grief,
  you watch and then take them into your hands;
  the luckless man commits himself to you,
  you, the orphan's certain help.

15 Break the power of the wicked, of the evil man,
  seek out his wickedness till there is none to be found!
16 Yahweh is king for ever and ever,
  the pagans are doomed to vanish from his country.

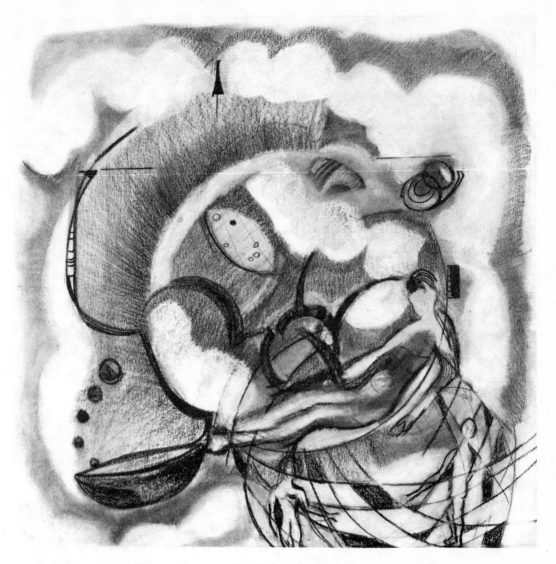

lurking unseen like a lion in his hide, / lurking to capture the poor man, / the poor man seized, he drags him away in his net.
(Psalm 10:9)

[17] Yahweh, you listen to the wants of the humble,
   you bring strength to their hearts, you grant them a hearing,
[18] judging in favor of the orphaned and exploited,
   so that earthborn man may strike fear no longer.

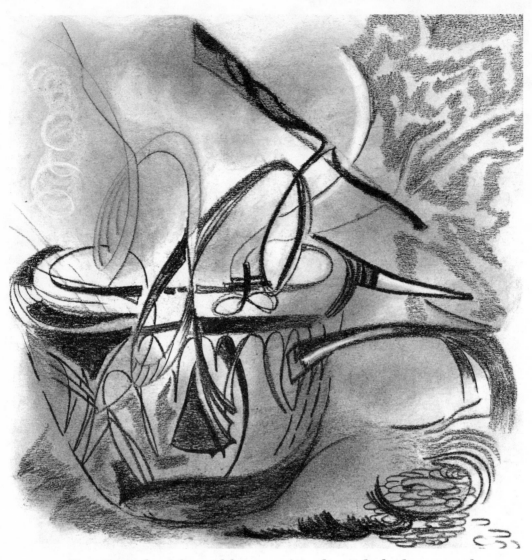

He rains coals of fire and brimstone on the wicked, / he serves them a scorching wind to swallow down.
(*Psalm* 11:6)

Psalm 11

For the choirmaster   Of David

THE CONFIDENCE OF THE VIRTUOUS

[1] In Yahweh I take shelter.
How can you say to me,
"Bird, fly back to your mountain:

[2] "see how the wicked are bending their bows
and fitting their arrows to the string,
ready to shoot the upright from the shadows.
[3] When foundations fall to ruin, what can the virtuous do?"
[4] Yahweh is in his holy Temple,
Yahweh whose throne is in heaven;
his eyes look down at the world,
his searching gaze scans all mankind.

[5] The virtuous and the wicked are under Yahweh's scrutiny,
and his soul hates anyone who loves brutality.
[6] He rains coals of fire and brimstone on the wicked,
he serves them a scorching wind to swallow down.
[7] Yahweh is righteous, he loves virtue,
upright men will contemplate his face.

Save us, Yahweh! There are no devout men left, / fidelity has vanished from mankind.
(Psalm 12:1)

Psalm 12

For the choirmaster   For the octachord   Psalm   Of David

AGAINST A DECEITFUL WORLD

[1] Save us, Yahweh! there are no devout men left,
fidelity has vanished from mankind.
[2] All they do is lie to one another,
flattering lips, talk from a double heart.

[3] May Yahweh slice off every flattering lip,
each tongue so glib with boasts,
[4] those who say, "In our tongue lies our strength,
our lips have the advantage; who can master us?"

[5] "For the plundered poor, for the needy who groan,
now will I act," says Yahweh.
"I will grant them the safety they sigh for."

[6] The words of Yahweh are without alloy,
nature's silver coming from the earth seven times refined.
[7] And you, Yahweh, hold us in your keeping,
against that breed protect us always.
[8] The wicked prowl on every side,
baseness stands high among the sons of men.

How much longer will you forget me? Yahweh? For ever? / How much longer will you hide your face from me?
(*Psalm 13:1*)

Psalm 13

For the choirmaster   Psalm   Of David

A CONFIDENT APPEAL

[1] How much longer will you forget me, Yahweh? For ever?
How much longer will you hide your face from me?
[2] How much longer must I endure grief in my soul,
and sorrow in my heart by day and by night?
How much longer must my enemy have the upper hand of me?
[3] Look and answer me, Yahweh my God!

Give my eyes light, or I shall sleep in death,
[4] and my enemy will say, "I have beaten him,"
and my oppressors have the joy of seeing me stumble.
[5] But I for my part rely on your love, Yahweh;
let my heart rejoice in your saving help.
Let me sing to Yahweh for the goodness he has shown me.

Yahweh is looking down from heaven / at the sons of men, / to see if a single one is wise, / if a single one is seeking God.
(Psalm 14:2)

Psalm 14

For the choirmaster   Of David

THE GODLESS MEN

[1] The fool says in his heart,
  "There is no God!"
 Their deeds are corrupt and vile,
  there is not one good man left.
[2] Yahweh is looking down from heaven
  at the sons of men,
 to see if a single one is wise,
  if a single one is seeking God.

[3] All have turned aside,
  all alike are tainted;
 there is not one good man left,
  not a single one.

[4] Are they so ignorant, all these evil men
  who swallow my people
 as though they were eating bread,
  and never invoke Yahweh?

[5] They will be struck with fear,
  fear without reason,
 since God takes the side of the virtuous:
[6] deride as you may the poor man's hopes,
  Yahweh is his shelter.

[7] Who will bring Israel salvation from Zion?
 When Yahweh brings his people home,
 what joy for Jacob, what happiness for Israel!

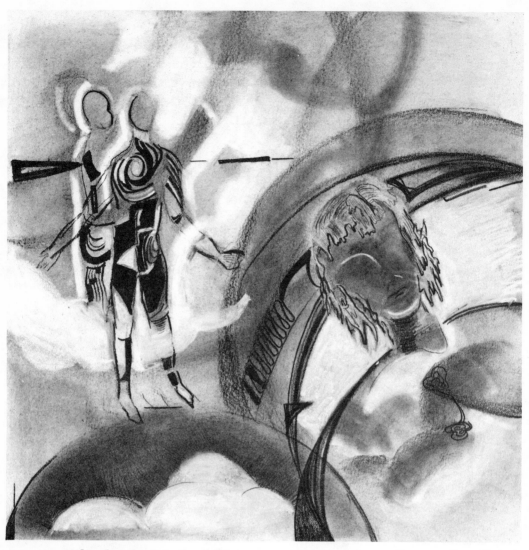

Yahweh, who has the right to enter your tent, / or to live on your holy mountain?
(Psalm 15:1)

Psalm 15

THE GUEST OF YAHWEH

[1] Yahweh, who has the right to enter your tent,
   or to live on your holy mountain?

[2] The man whose way of life is blameless,
   who always does what is right,
   who speaks the truth from his heart,
[3] whose tongue is not used for slander,

   who does no wrong to his fellow,
   casts no discredit on his neighbor,
[4] looks with contempt on the reprobate,
   but honors those who fear Yahweh;

   who stands by his pledge at any cost,
[5] does not ask interest on loans,
   and cannot be bribed to victimize the ·innocent.
   —If a man does all this, nothing can ever shake him.

Look after me, God, I take shelter in you.
(Psalm 16:1)

Psalm 16

Miktam   Of David

YAHWEH, MY HERITAGE

1   Look after me, God, I take shelter in you.

2   To Yahweh you say, "My Lord,
      you are my fortune, nothing else but you,"
3   yet to those pagan deities in the land,
      "My princes, all my pleasure is in you."

4 Their idols teem, after these they run:
 shall I pour their blood libations?—not I!
 Take their names on my lips?—never!
5 Yahweh, my heritage, my cup,
 you, and you only, hold my lot secure;
6 the measuring line marks out delightful places for me,
 for me the heritage is superb indeed.
7 I bless Yahweh, who is my counselor,
 and in the night my inmost self instructs me;
8 I keep Yahweh before me always,
 for with him at my right hand nothing can shake me.

9 So my heart exults, my very soul rejoices,
 my body, too, will rest securely,
10 for you will not abandon my soul to Sheol,
 nor allow the one you love to see the Pit;
11 you will reveal the path of life to me,
 give me unbounded joy in your presence,
 and at your right hand everlasting pleasures.

guard me like the pupil of your eye; / hide me in the shadow of your wings
(*Psalm 17:8*)

Psalm 17

Prayer   Of David

THE INNOCENT MAN PLEADS HIS CAUSE

¹   Yahweh, hear the plea of virtue,
  listen to my appeal,
lend an ear to my prayer,
  my lips free from dishonesty.
²   From your presence will my sentence come,
  your eyes are fixed on what is right,

³ You probe my heart, examine me at night,
 you test me yet find nothing, no murmuring from me:
⁴ my mouth has never sinned ·as most men's do.

 No, I have treasured the words from your lips;
⁵ in the path prescribed ·walking deliberately
 in your footsteps, so that my feet do not slip.

⁶ I invoke you, God, and you answer me;
 turn your ear to me, hear what I say,
⁷ display your marvelous kindness, savior of fugitives!

 From those who revolt against you
⁸ guard me like the pupil of your eye;
 hide me in the shadow of your wings
⁹ from the onslaughts of the wicked.

 My enemies cluster around me, breathing hostility;
¹⁰ entrenched in their fat, their mouths utter
¹¹ arrogant claims; ·now they are closing in,
 they have eyes for nothing but to see me overthrown.
¹² They look like a lion eager to tear to pieces,
 like a young lion crouching in its hide.

¹³ Rise, Yahweh, subdue him face to face,
 rescue my soul from the wicked with your sword,
¹⁴ with your hand, Yahweh, rescue me from men,
 from the sort of men whose lot is here and now.

 Cram their bellies from your stores,
  give them all the sons that they could wish for,
 let them have a surplus to leave their children!
¹⁵ For me the reward of virtue is to see your face,
 and, on waking, to gaze my fill on your likeness.

Psalm 18

For the choirmaster. Of David, the servant of Yahweh, who addressed the words of this song to Yahweh at the time when Yahweh delivered him from the power of his enemies and of Saul. He said:

SONG OF TRIUMPH FOR THE KING

[1] I love you, Yahweh, my strength
(my savior, you rescue me from violence).
[2] Yahweh is my rock and my bastion,
my deliverer is my God.

I take shelter in him, my rock,
my shield, my horn of salvation,
my stronghold and my refuge.
From violence you rescue me.
[3] He is to be praised; on Yahweh I call
and am saved from my enemies.

[4] The waves of death encircled me,
the torrents of Belial burst on me;
[5] the cords of Sheol girdled me,
the snares of death were before me.

[6] In my distress I called to Yahweh
and to my God I cried;
from his Temple he heard my voice,
my cry came to his ears.

[7] Then the earth quivered and quaked,
the foundations of the mountains trembled
(they quivered because he was angry);
[8] from his nostrils a smoke ascended,
and from his mouth a fire that consumed
(live embers were kindled at it).

[9] He bent the heavens and came down,
a dark cloud under his feet;
[10] he mounted a cherub and flew,
and soared on the wings of the wind.

[11] Darkness he made a veil to surround him,
his tent a watery darkness, dense cloud;
[12] before him a flash enkindled
hail and fiery embers.

I love you, Yahweh, my strength / (my savior, you rescue me from violence).
(Psalm 18:1)

[13] Yahweh thundered from heaven,
   the Most High made his voice heard;
[14] he let his arrows fly and scattered them,
   launched the lightnings and routed them.

[15] The bed of the seas was revealed,
   the foundations of the world were laid bare,
   at your muttered threat, Yahweh,
   at the blast of your nostril's breath.

¹⁶ He sends from on high and takes me,
   he draws me from deep waters,
¹⁷ he delivers me from my powerful enemy,
   from a foe too strong for me.

¹⁸ They assailed me on my day of disaster,
   but Yahweh was my support;
¹⁹ he freed me, set me at large,
   he rescued me, since he loves me.

²⁰ Yahweh requites me as I act justly,
   as my hands are pure so he repays me,
²¹ since I have kept the ways of Yahweh,
   nor fallen away from my God.

²² His judgments are all before me,
   his statutes I have not put from me;
²³ I am blameless in his presence,
   I keep sin at arm's length.

²⁴ And Yahweh repays me as I act justly,
   as my purity is in his sight.
²⁵ Faithful you are with the faithful,
   blameless with the blameless,

²⁶ pure with the one who is pure,
   but crafty with the devious,
²⁷ you save a people that is humble,
   and humiliate eyes that are haughty.

²⁸ Yahweh, you yourself are my lamp,
   my God lights up my darkness;
²⁹ with you I storm the barbican,
   with my God I leap the rampart.

³⁰ This God, his way is blameless;
   the word of Yahweh is without dross.
   He it is who is the shield
   of all who take shelter in him.

³¹ Who else is God but Yahweh,
   who else a rock save our God?
³² This God who girds me with strength
   and makes my way without blame,

³³ who makes my feet like the hinds'
   and holds me from falling on the heights,
³⁴ who trains my hands for battle,
   my arms to bend a bow of bronze.

[35] You give me your saving shield
   (your right hand upholds me), with care you train me,
[36] wide room you make for my steps under me,
   my feet have never faltered.

[37] I pursue my enemies and overtake them,
   nor turn back till an end is made of them;
[38] I strike them down, and they cannot rise,
   they fall, they are under my feet.

[39] You have girt me with strength for the fight,
   bent down my assailants beneath me,
[40] made my enemies turn their backs to me;
   and those who hate me I destroy.

[41] They cry out, there is no one to save,
   to Yahweh, but there is no reply;
[42] I crush them fine as dust before the wind,
   trample them like the mud of the streets.

[43] You deliver me from a people in revolt,
   you place me at the head of the nations,
   a people I did not know are now my servants,

[44] foreigners come wooing my favor,
   no sooner do they hear than they obey me,
[45] foreigners grow faint of heart,
   they come trembling out of their fastnesses.

[46] Life to Yahweh! Blessed be my rock!
   Exalted be the God of my salvation,
[47] the God who gives me vengeance
   and subjects the peoples to me,

[48] who rescues me from my raging enemies.
   You lift me high above those who attack me,
   you deliver me from the man of violence.

[49] For this I will praise you, Yahweh, among the heathen
   and sing praise to your name.

[50] His king he saves and saves again,
   displays his love for his anointed,
   for David and his heirs for ever.

Psalm 19

For the choirmaster   Psalm   Of David

YAHWEH, THE SUN OF RIGHTEOUSNESS

¹ The heavens declare the glory of God,
  the vault of heaven proclaims his handiwork;
² day discourses of it to day,
  night to night hands on the knowledge.

³ No utterance at all, no speech,
  no sound that anyone can hear;
⁴ yet their voice goes out through all the earth,
  and their message to the ends of the world.

High above, he pitched a tent for the sun,
⁵ who comes out of his pavilion like a bridegroom,
  exulting like a hero to run his race.

⁶ He has his rising on the edge of heaven,
  the end of his course is its furthest edge,
  and nothing can escape his heat.

⁷   The Law of Yahweh is perfect,
        new life for the soul;
    the decree of Yahweh is trustworthy,
        wisdom for the simple.

⁸   The precepts of Yahweh are upright,
        joy for the heart;
    the commandment of Yahweh is clear,
        light for the eyes.

⁹   The fear of Yahweh is pure,
        lasting for ever;
    the judgments of Yahweh are true,
        righteous, every one,

¹⁰   more desirable than gold,
        even than the finest gold;
    his words are sweeter than honey,
        even than honey that drips from the comb.

¹¹   Thus your servant is formed by them,
        observance brings great reward.
¹²   But who can detect his own failings?
        Wash out my hidden faults.

The heavens declare the glory of God, / the vault of heaven proclaims his handiwork;
(Psalm 19:1)

13 And from pride preserve your servant,
       never let it dominate me.
    So shall I be above reproach,
       free from grave sin.

14 May the words of my mouth always find favor,
       and the whispering of my heart,
    in your presence, Yahweh,
       my Rock, my Redeemer!

May Yahweh answer you in time of trouble, / may the name of the God of Jacob protect you!
(*Psalm 20:1*)

Psalm 20

For the choirmaster   Psalm   Of David

PRAYER FOR THE KING

[1] May Yahweh answer you in time of trouble,
  may the name of the God of Jacob protect you!

[2] May he send you help from the sanctuary,
  give you support from Zion,
[3] remember all your oblations
  and find your holocaust acceptable;   *Pause*
[4] may he grant you your heart's desire,
  and crown all your plans with success;
[5] may we shout with joy for your victory,
  and plant our banners in the name of our God!

May Yahweh grant all your petitions!

[6] Now I know that Yahweh
  saves his anointed,
  and answers him from his holy heaven
  with mighty victories from his own right hand.

[7] Some boast of chariots, some of horses,
  but we boast about the name of Yahweh our God;
[8] theirs to crumple and fall,
  but we shall stand, and stand firm!

[9] Yahweh, save the king,
  answer us when we call.

you will make them like a blazing furnace, / the day that you appear, / Yahweh will engulf them in his anger, / and fire will devour them;
(Psalm 21:9)

Psalm 21

For the choirmaster   Psalm   Of David

THANKSGIVING FOR THE KING

[1] Yahweh, the king rejoices in your power;
  what great joy your saving help gives him!
[2] You have granted him his heart's desire,
  not denied him what his lips entreated.   *Pause*

[3] For you have met him with choicest blessings,
  put a crown of pure gold on his head;
[4] he asked for life, and you gave it him,
  length of days for ever and ever.

[5] Great his glory through your saving help,
  you have loaded him with splendor and majesty;
[6] yes, you confer on him everlasting blessings,
  you gladden him with the joy of your presence.

[7] Yes, the king puts his trust in Yahweh,
  by grace of the Most High he reigns unshaken.

[8]   Your hand will unmask all your enemies,
    your right hand all who hate you;
[9]   you will make them like a blazing furnace,
      the day that you appear,

  Yahweh will engulf them in his anger,
    and fire will devour them;
[10] you will wipe their children from the earth,
  their descendants from among the sons of men.

[11] Plot though they do to harm you
  and weave their plan as they may, they cannot win;
[12] since you will make them turn tail,
  by shooting your arrows in their faces.
[13] Rise, Yahweh, in your power!
  We will sing and play in honor of your strength.

Psalm 22

For the choirmaster   To the "Doe of the Dawn"   Psalm   Of David

THE SUFFERINGS AND HOPE OF THE
VIRTUOUS MAN

[1] My God, my God, why have you deserted me?
How far from saving me, the words I groan!
[2] I call all day, my God, but you never answer,
all night long I call and cannot rest.
[3] Yet, Holy One, you
who make your home in the praises of Israel,
[4] in you our fathers put their trust,
they trusted and you rescued them;
[5] they called to you for help and they were saved,
they never trusted you in vain.

[6] Yet here am I, now more worm than man,
scorn of mankind, jest of the people,
[7] all who see me jeer at me,
they toss their heads and sneer,
[8] "He relied on Yahweh, let Yahweh save him!
If Yahweh is his friend, let Him rescue him!"

[9] Yet you drew me out of the womb,
you entrusted me to my mother's breasts;
[10] placed on your lap from my birth,
from my mother's womb you have been my God.
[11] Do not stand aside; trouble is near,
I have no one to help me!

[12] A herd of bulls surrounds me,
strong bulls of Bashan close in on me;
[13] their jaws are agape for me,
like lions tearing and roaring.

[14] I am like water draining away,
my bones are all disjointed,
my heart is like wax,
melting inside me;
[15a] my palate is drier than a potsherd
[15b] and my tongue is stuck to my jaw.

[16] A pack of dogs surrounds me,
a gang of villains closes me in;

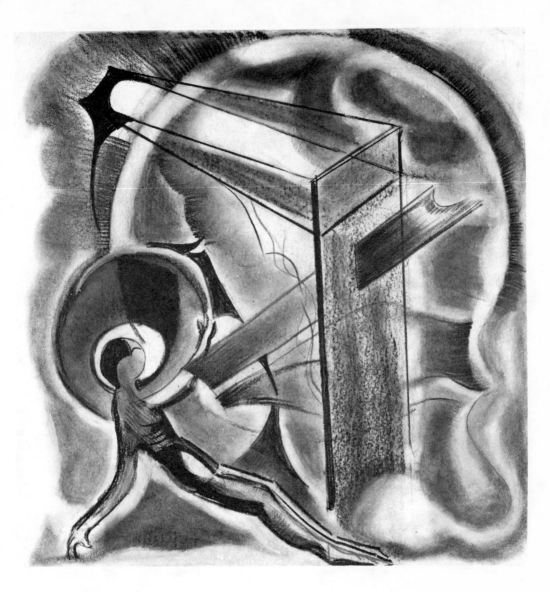

*My God, my God, why have you deserted me? / How far from saving
me, the words I groan!*
(Psalm 22:1)

they tie me hand and foot
[15c] and leave me lying in the dust of death.

[17] I can count every one of my bones,
and there they glare at me, gloating;
[18] they divide my garments among them
and cast lots for my clothes.

^{19} Do not stand aside, Yahweh.
O my strength, come quickly to my help;
^{20} rescue my soul from the sword,
my dear life from the paw of the dog,
^{21} save me from the lion's mouth,
my poor soul from the wild bulls' horns!

^{22} Then I shall proclaim your name to my brothers,
praise you in full assembly:
^{23} you who fear Yahweh, praise him!
Entire race of Jacob, glorify him!
Entire race of Israel, revere him!

^{24} For he has not despised
or disdained the poor man in his poverty,
has not hidden his face from him,
but has answered him when he called.

^{25} You are the theme of my praise in the Great Assembly,
I perform my vows in the presence of those who fear him.
^{26} The poor will receive as much as they want to eat.
Those who seek Yahweh will praise him.
Long life to their hearts!

^{27} The whole earth, from end to end, will remember and come back to
Yahweh;
all the families of the nations will bow down before him.
^{28} For Yahweh reigns, the ruler of nations!
^{29} Before him all the prosperous of the earth will bow down,
before him will bow all who go down to the dust.
^{30} And my soul will live for him, ·my children will serve him;
^{31} men will proclaim the Lord to generations ·still to come,
his righteousness to a people yet unborn. All this he has done.

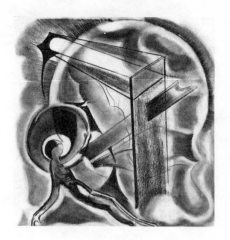

Yahweh is my shepherd, / I lack nothing.
(Psalm 23:1)

Psalm 23

Psalm Of David

THE GOOD SHEPHERD

¹ Yahweh is my shepherd,
   I lack nothing.

² In meadows of green grass he lets me lie.
  To the waters of repose he leads me;
³   there he revives my soul.

  He guides me by paths of virtue
    for the sake of his name.

⁴ Though I pass through a gloomy valley,
    I fear no harm;
  beside me your rod and your staff
    are there, to hearten me.

⁵ You prepare a table before me
    under the eyes of my enemies;
  you anoint my head with oil,
    my cup brims over.

⁶ Ah, how goodness and kindness pursue me,
    every day of my life;
  my home, the house of Yahweh,
    as long as I live!

To Yahweh belong earth and all it holds, / the world and all who live in it;
(Psalm 24:1)

Psalm 24

Psalm   Of   David

ANTIPHONAL PSALM FOR SOLEMN ENTRY
INTO THE SANCTUARY

[1] To Yahweh belong earth and all it holds,
the world and all who live in it;
[2] he himself founded it on the ocean,
based it firmly on the nether sea.

[3] Who has the right to climb the mountain of Yahweh,
who the right to stand in his holy place?
[4] He whose hands are clean, whose heart is pure,
whose soul does not pay homage to worthless things
and who never swears to a lie.

[5] The blessing of Yahweh is his,
and vindication from God his savior.
[6] Such are the people who seek him,
who seek your presence, God of Jacob!   *Pause*

[7] Gates, raise your arches,
rise, you ancient doors,
let the king of glory in!

[8] Who is this king of glory?
Yahweh the strong, the valiant,
Yahweh valiant in battle!

[9] Gates, raise your arches,
rise, you ancient doors,
let the king of glory in!

[10] Who is this king of glory?
He is Yahweh Sabaoth,
King of glory, he!   *Pause*

Psalm 25

Of David

PRAYER IN DANGER

¹ To you, Yahweh, I lift up my soul,
² O my God.

I rely on you, do not let me be shamed,
do not let my enemies gloat over me!
³ No, those who hope in you are never shamed,
shame awaits disappointed traitors.

⁴ Yahweh, make your ways known to me,
teach me your paths.
⁵ Set me in the way of your truth, and teach me,
for you are the God who saves me.

All day long I hope in you
⁷ᶜ because of your goodness, Yahweh.
⁶ Remember your kindness, Yahweh,
your love, that you showed long ago.
⁷ᵃ Do not remember the sins of my youth;
⁷ᵇ but rather, with your love remember me.

⁸ Yahweh is so good, so upright,
he teaches the way to sinners;
⁹ in all that is right he guides the humble,
and instructs the poor in his way.

¹⁰ All Yahweh's paths are love and truth
for those who keep his covenant and his decrees.
¹¹ For the sake of your name, Yahweh,
forgive my guilt, for it is great.

¹² Everyone who fears Yahweh
will be taught the course a man should choose;
¹³ his soul will live in prosperity,
his children have the land for their own.
¹⁴ The close secret of Yahweh belongs to them who fear him,
his covenant also, to bring them knowledge.

¹⁵ My eyes are always on Yahweh,
for he releases my feet from the net.
¹⁶ Turn to me, take pity on me,
alone and wretched as I am!

¹⁷ Relieve the distress of my heart,
free me from my sufferings.

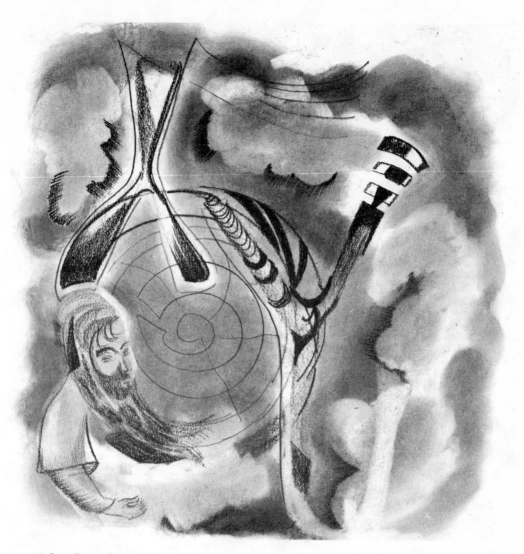

Yahweh, make your ways known to me, / teach me your paths.
(Psalm 25:4)

[18] See my misery and pain,
   forgive all my sins!

[19] See how my enemies multiply,
   and how violent their hatred has grown.
[20] Watch over my soul, rescue me;
   let me not be shamed: I take shelter in you.
[21] Let innocence and integrity be my protection,
   since my hope is in you, Yahweh.

   Redeem Israel, God,
   from all his troubles.

for your love is before my eyes, / and I live my life in loyalty to you.
(Psalm 26:3)

Psalm 26

Of David

PRAYER OF THE BLAMELESS

[1] Yahweh, be my judge!
I go my way in my innocence,
My trust in Yahweh never wavers.
[2] Test me, Yahweh, and probe me,
put me to the trial, loins and heart;
[3] for your love is before my eyes,
and I live my life in loyalty to you.

[4] No sitting with wastrels for me,
no associating with hypocrites;
[5] I hate the society of evil men,
I refuse to sit down with the wicked.

[6] I wash my hands in innocence
and join the procession around your altar,
[7] singing a hymn of thanksgiving,
proclaiming all your wonders.
[8] I love the house where you live,
the place where your glory makes its home.

[9] Do not let my soul share the fate of sinners,
or my life the doom of men of blood,
[10] men with guilt on their hands,
whose right hands are heavy with bribes.

[11] But I live my life in innocence,
redeem me, Yahweh, take pity on me;
[12] my foot is set on the right path,
I bless you, Yahweh, at the Assemblies.

Psalm 27

Of David

IN GOD'S COMPANY THERE IS NO FEAR

¹ Yahweh is my light and my salvation,
    whom need I fear?
Yahweh is the fortress of my life,
    of whom should I be afraid?
² When evil men advance against me
    to devour my flesh,
they, my opponents, my enemies,
    are the ones who stumble and fall.

³ Though an army pitched camp against me,
    my heart would not fear;
though war were waged against me,
    my trust would still be firm.

⁴ One thing I ask of Yahweh,
    one thing I seek:
to live in the house of Yahweh
    all the days of my life,
to enjoy the sweetness of Yahweh
    and to consult him in his Temple.
⁵ For he shelters me under his awning
    in times of trouble;
he hides me deep in his tent,
    sets me high on a rock.

⁶ And now my head is held high
    over the enemies who surround me,
in his tent I will offer
    exultant sacrifice.

I will sing, I will play for Yahweh!

⁷ Yahweh, hear my voice as I cry!
    Pity me! Answer me!
⁸ My heart has said of you,
    "Seek his face."
Yahweh, I do seek your face;
⁹ do not hide your face from me.

Do not repulse your servant in anger;
    you are my help.

For he shelters me under his awning / in times of trouble; / he hides me deep in his tent, / sets me high on a rock.
(*Psalm 27:5*)

Never leave me, never desert me,
   God, my savior!
[10] If my father and mother desert me,
   Yahweh will care for me still.

[11] Yahweh, teach me your way,
   lead me in the path of integrity
      because of my enemies;

[12] do not abandon me to the will of my foes—
   false witnesses have risen against me,
     and breathe out violence.

[13] This I believe: I shall see the goodness of Yahweh,
   in the land of the living.
[14] Put your hope in Yahweh, be strong, let your heart be bold,
   put your hope in Yahweh.

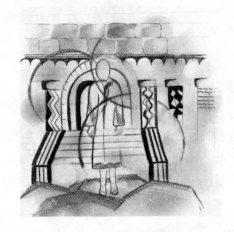

Yahweh is my strength, my shield, / my heart puts its trust in him; / I have been helped, my flesh has bloomed again, / I thank him with all my heart.
(Psalm 28:7)

Psalm 28

Of David

PETITION AND THANKSGIVING

[1] I cry to you, Yahweh,
   my Rock! Do not be deaf to me,
for if you are silent, I shall go
   down to the Pit like the rest.

[2] Hear my voice, raised in petition,
   as I cry to you for help,
as I raise my hands, Yahweh,
   toward your Holy of Holies.

[3] Do not drag me away with the wicked,
   away with the evil men
who talk of peace to their neighbors
   while malice is in their hearts.

[4] Repay them for their actions, Yahweh,
   for the evil they commit,
for their handiwork repay them,
   let them have what they deserve!

[5] How blind they are to the works of Yahweh,
   to his own handiwork!
May he pull them down and not rebuild them!

[6] Blessed be Yahweh, for he hears
   the sound of my petition!

[7] Yahweh is my strength, my shield,
   my heart puts its trust in him;
I have been helped, my flesh has bloomed again,
   I thank him with all my heart.

[8] Yahweh is the strength of his people,
a saving fortress for his anointed.
[9] Save your people! Bless your heritage!
Shepherd them; carry them for ever!

The voice of Yahweh over the waters! / Yahweh over the multitudinous waters!
(*Psalm 29:3*)

Psalm 29

Psalm Of David

HYMN TO THE LORD OF THE STORM

[1] Pay tribute to Yahweh, you sons of God,
  tribute to Yahweh of glory and power,
[2] tribute to Yahweh of the glory of his name,
  worship Yahweh in his sacred court.

[3a] The voice of Yahweh over the waters!
[3c] Yahweh over the multitudinous waters!
[4] The voice of Yahweh in power!
  The voice of Yahweh in splendor!

[5] The voice of Yahweh shatters the cedars,
  Yahweh shatters the cedars of Lebanon,
[6] making Lebanon leap like a calf,
  Sirion like a young wild bull.

[7] The voice of Yahweh sharpens lightning shafts!

[8] The voice of Yahweh sets the wilderness shaking.
  Yahweh shakes the wilderness of Kadesh.
[9a] The voice of Yahweh sets the terebinths shuddering,
[9b] stripping the forests bare.

[3b] The God of glory thunders.
[9c] In his palace everything cries, "Glory!"
[10] Yahweh sat enthroned for the Flood,
  Yahweh sits enthroned as a king for ever.

[11] Yahweh gives strength to his people,
  Yahweh blesses his people with peace.

Yahweh, you have brought my soul up from Sheol, / of all those who go down to the Pit you have revived me.
(*Psalm 30:3*)

Psalm 30

Psalm   Canticle for the Dedication of the House   Of David

THANKSGIVING AFTER MORTAL DANGER

1   High praise, Yahweh, I give you, for you have helped me up,
   and not let my enemies gloat over me.
2   Yahweh, my God, I cried to you for help, and you have healed me.
3 Yahweh, you have brought my soul up from Sheol,
   of all those who go down to the Pit you have revived me.

4   Play music in Yahweh's honor, you devout,
   remember his holiness, and praise him.
5 His anger lasts a moment, his favor a lifetime;
   in the evening, a spell of tears, in the morning, shouts of joy.

6   In my prosperity, I used to say,
   "Nothing can ever shake me!"
7 Your favor, Yahweh, stood me on a peak impregnable;
   but then you hid your face and I was terrified.

8   Yahweh, I call to you,
   I beg my God to pity me,
9 "What do you gain by my blood if I go down to the Pit?
   Can the dust praise you or proclaim your faithfulness?

10   "Hear, Yahweh, take pity on me;
   Yahweh, help me!"
11 You have turned my mourning into dancing,
   you have stripped off my sackcloth and wrapped me in gladness;
12 and now my heart, silent no longer, will play you music;
   Yahweh, my God, I will praise you for ever.

Psalm 31

For the choirmaster   Psalm   Of David

PRAYER IN TIME OF ORDEAL

¹ In you, Yahweh, I take shelter;
never let me be disgraced.
In your righteousness deliver me, rescue me,
² turn your ear to me, make haste!

Be a sheltering rock for me,
a walled fortress to save me!
³ For you are my rock, my fortress;
for the sake of your name, guide me, lead me!

⁴ Pull me out of the net they have spread for me,
for you are my refuge;
⁵ into your hands I commit my spirit,
you have redeemed me, Yahweh.

⁶ God of truth, ·you hate
those who serve worthless idols;
but I put my trust in Yahweh:
⁷ I will exult, and rejoice in your love!

You, who have seen my wretchedness,
and known the miseries of my soul,
⁸ have not handed me over to the enemy,
you have given my feet space and to spare.

⁹ Take pity on me, Yahweh,
    I am in trouble now.
Grief wastes away my eye,
    my throat, my inmost parts.

¹⁰ For my life is worn out with sorrow,
    my years with sighs;
my strength yields under misery,
    my bones are wasting away.

¹¹ To every one of my oppressors
    I am contemptible,
loathsome to my neighbors,
    to my friends a thing of fear.

Those who see me in the street
    hurry past me;

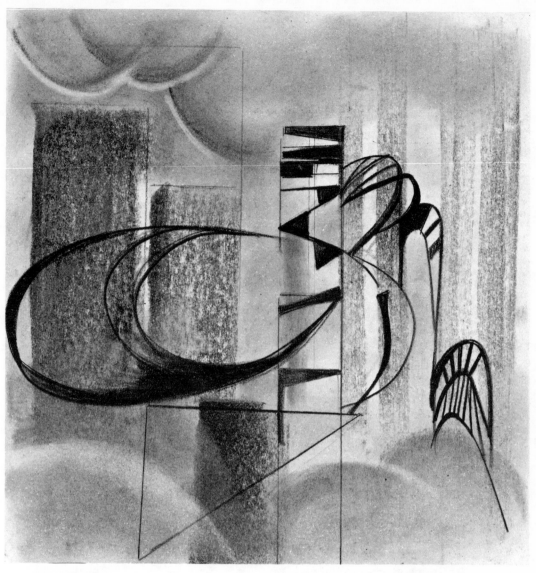

Blessed be Yahweh, who performs / marvels of love for me / (in a fortress-city)!
(Psalm 31:21)

¹² I am forgotten, as good as dead in their hearts,
    something discarded.

¹³ I hear their endless slanders,
    threats from every quarter,
  as they combine against me,
    plotting to take my life.

¹⁴ But I put my trust in you, Yahweh,
    I say, "You are my God."
¹⁵ My days are in your hand, rescue me
    from the hands of my enemies and persecutors;
¹⁶ let your face smile on your servant,
    save me in your love.

¹⁷ I invoke you, Yahweh; do not let me be disgraced
    let the disgrace fall on the wicked!
  May they go speechless to Sheol,
¹⁸   their lying lips struck dumb
  for those insolent slurs on the virtuous,
    for that arrogance and contempt.

¹⁹ Yahweh, how great your goodness,
    reserved for those who fear you,
  bestowed on those who take shelter in you,
    for all mankind to see!

²⁰ Safe in your presence you hide them
    far from the wiles of men;
  inside your tent you shelter them
    far from the war of tongues.

²¹ Blessed be Yahweh, who performs
    marvels of love for me
    (in a fortress-city)!
²² In my alarm I exclaimed,
    "I have been snatched out of your sight!"
  Yet you heard my petition
    when I called to you for help.

²² Love Yahweh, all you devout:
    Yahweh, protector of the faithful,
  will repay the arrogant
    with interest.
²⁴ Be strong, let your heart be bold,
    all you who hope in Yahweh!

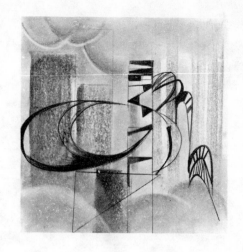

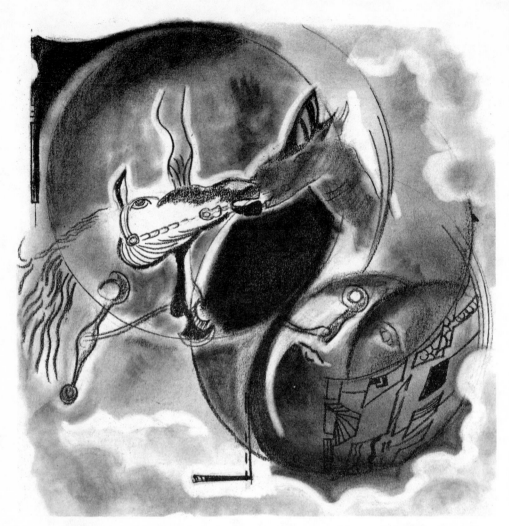

Do not be like senseless horse or mule / that need bit and bridle to curb their spirit / (to let you get near them).
(Psalm 32:9)

Psalm 32

Of David Poem

CANDID ADMISSION OF SIN

[1] Happy the man whose fault is forgiven,
  whose sin is blotted out;
[2] happy the man whom Yahweh
  accuses of no guilt,
  whose spirit is incapable of deceit!

[3] All the time I kept silent, my bones were wasting away
  with groans, day in, day out;
[4] day and night your hand
  lay heavy on me;
my heart grew parched as stubble
  in summer drought. *Pause*

[5] At last I admitted to you I had sinned;
  no longer concealing my guilt,
I said, "I will go to Yahweh
  and confess my fault."
And you, you have forgiven the wrong I did,
  have pardoned my sin. *Pause*

[6] That is why each of your servants prays to you
  in time of trouble;
even if floods come rushing down,
  they will never reach him.
[7] You are a hiding place for me,
  you guard me when in trouble,
you surround me with songs of deliverance. *Pause*

[8] I will instruct you, and teach you the way to go;
I will watch over you and be your adviser.

[9] Do not be like senseless horse or mule
that need bit and bridle to curb their spirit
(to let you get near them).

[10] Many torments await the wicked,
  but grace enfolds the man who trusts in Yahweh.

[11]   Rejoice in Yahweh,
  exult, you virtuous,
  shout for joy, all upright hearts.

Psalm 33

[1] Shout for joy to Yahweh, all virtuous men,
praise comes well from upright hearts;
[2] give thanks to Yahweh on the lyre,
play to him on the ten-string harp;
[3] sing a new song in his honor,
play with all your skill as you acclaim him!
[4] The word of Yahweh is integrity itself,
all he does is done faithfully;
[5] he loves virtue and justice,
Yahweh's love fills the earth.

[6] By the word of Yahweh the heavens were made,
their whole array by the breath of his mouth;
[7] he collects the ocean waters as though in a wineskin,
he stores the deeps in cellars.
[8] Let the whole world fear Yahweh,
let all who live on earth revere him!
[9] He spoke, and it was created;
he commanded, and there it stood.

[10] Yahweh thwarts the plans of nations,
frustrates the intentions of peoples;
[11] but Yahweh's plans hold good for ever,
the intentions of his heart from age to age.
[12] Happy the nation whose God is Yahweh,
the people he has chosen for his heritage.

[13] Yahweh looks down from heaven,
he sees the whole human race;
[14] from where he sits he watches
all who live on the earth,
[15] he who molds every heart
and takes note of all men do.

[16] A large army will not keep a king safe,
nor does the hero escape by his great strength;
[17] it is delusion to rely on the horse for safety,
for all its power, it cannot save.

[18] But see how the eye of Yahweh is on those who fear him,
on those who rely on his love,

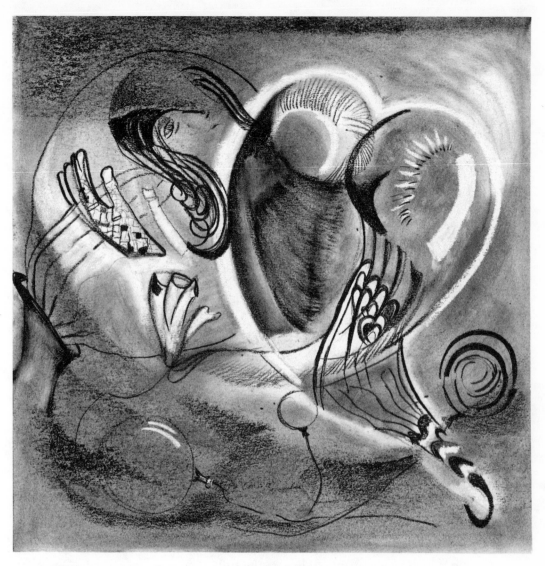

our hearts rejoice in him, / we trust in his holy name.
(Psalm 33:21)

[19] to rescue their souls from death
and keep them alive in famine.

[20] Our soul awaits Yahweh,
he is our help and shield;
[21] our hearts rejoice in him,
we trust in his holy name.
[22] Yahweh, let your love rest on us
as our hope has rested in you.

Psalm 34

*Of David. When after pretending to be mad in front of Abimelech,
he was dismissed by him and made his escape*

IN PRAISE OF GOD'S JUSTICE

¹ I will bless Yahweh at all times,
  his praise shall be on my lips continually;
² my soul glories in Yahweh,
  let the humble hear and rejoice.

³ Proclaim with me the greatness of Yahweh,
  together let us extol his name.
⁴ I seek Yahweh, and he answers me
  and frees me from all my fears.

⁵ Every face turned to him grows brighter
  and is never ashamed.
⁶ A cry goes up from the poor man, and Yahweh hears,
  and helps him in all his troubles.

⁷ The angel of Yahweh pitches camp
  around those who fear him; and he keeps them safe.
⁸ How good Yahweh is—only taste and see!
  Happy the man who takes shelter in him.

⁹ Fear Yahweh, you his holy ones:
  those who fear him want for nothing.
¹⁰ The young lion may go empty and hungry,
  but those who seek Yahweh lack nothing good.

¹¹ Come, my sons, listen to me,
  I will teach you the fear of Yahweh.
¹² Which of you wants to live to the full,
  who loves long life and enjoyment of prosperity?

¹³ Malice must be banished from your tongue,
  deceitful conversation from your lips;
¹⁴ never yield to evil, practice good,
  seek peace, pursue it.

¹⁶ The face of Yahweh frowns on evil men,
  to wipe their memory from the earth;
¹⁵ the eyes of Yahweh are turned toward the virtuous,
  his ears to their cry.

¹⁷ They cry for help and Yahweh hears
  and rescues them from all their troubles;

The young lion may go empty and hungry, / but those who seek Yahweh lack nothing good.
(Psalm 34:10)

[18] Yahweh is near to the brokenhearted,
he helps those whose spirit is crushed.

[19] Hardships in plenty beset the virtuous man,
but Yahweh rescues him from them all;
[20] taking care of every bone,
Yahweh will not let one be broken.

[21] Evil will bring death to the wicked,
those who hate the virtuous will have to pay;
[22] while Yahweh himself ransoms the souls of his servants,
and those who take shelter in him have nothing to pay.

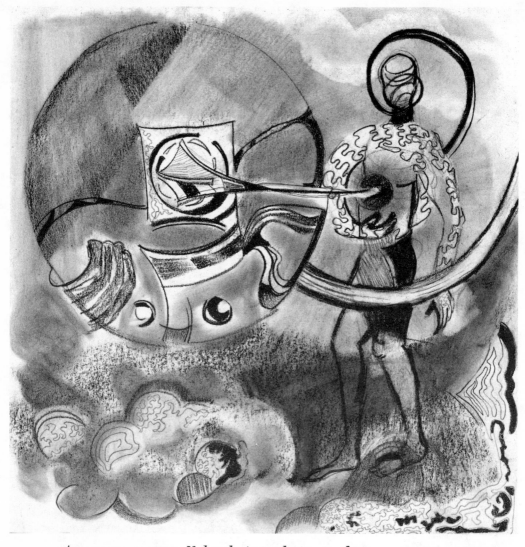

Accuse my accusers, Yahweh, / attack my attackers;
(Psalm 35:1)

Psalm 35

Of David

PRAYER OF A VIRTUOUS MAN UNDER OPPRESSION

¹ Accuse my accusers, Yahweh,
    attack my attackers;
² grip shield and buckler,
    up, and help me;
³ brandish lance and pike
    in the faces of my pursuers.
Tell my soul, "I am your salvation."

⁴ Shame and dishonor on those
    who are out to kill me!
Back with them! Cover with confusion
    those who plot my downfall!
⁵ May they be like chaff before the wind,
    with the angel of Yahweh to chase them!
⁶ May their way be dark and slippery,
    with the angel of Yahweh to hound them!

⁷ Unprovoked they spread their net for me,
    they dug a pit for me;
⁸ but Ruin creeps on them unawares,
    the net they have spread will catch them instead,
    and into their own pit will they fall.

⁹ Then my soul will rejoice in Yahweh,
    exult that he has saved me.
¹⁰ All my bones will exclaim, "Yahweh,
    who can compare with you
in rescuing the poor man from the stronger,
    the needy from the man who exploits him?"

¹¹ Lying witnesses take the stand,
    questioning me on things I know nothing about;
¹² they repay my kindness with evil,
    there is desolation in my soul.

¹³ Yet, when they were sick, I put sackcloth on,
    I humbled my soul with fasting,
murmuring prayers to my own breast
¹⁴   as though for a friend or brother;
and, like a person mourning his mother,
    went about dejected and sorrowing.

¹⁵ Now I have fallen, they crowd around delighted,
    flocking to jeer at me;
  strangers I never even knew
    with loud cries tear me to pieces,
¹⁶ riddling me with gibe after gibe,
    grinding their teeth at me.

¹⁷ How much longer, Lord, will you look on?
  Rescue my soul from their onslaughts,
    my dear life from these lions.
¹⁸ I will give thanks in the Great Assembly,
    praise you where the people throng.

¹⁹ Do not let my lying enemies
    gloat over me,
  do not let those who hate me for no reason
    exchange sly glances.

²⁰ Peace is not what they discuss
    with the peace-loving people of the land;
  they think out false accusations,
²¹   their mouths wide to accuse me,
  "Aha! Aha!" they say,
    "With our own eyes we saw it!"

²² Now break your silence, Yahweh, you were looking too,
    Lord, do not stand aside,
²³ up, wake up, come to my defense,
    Lord my God side with me!
²⁴ Yahweh my God, you are righteous, so give verdict for me,
    and do not let them gloat over me.

²⁵ Do not let them think, "Just as we hoped!"
    Do not let them say, "Now we have got him down!"
²⁶ Shame and dishonor on all
    who gloat over my misfortune;
  shame and discredit cover all
    who profit at my expense!

²⁷ But shouts of joy and gladness for all
    who take pleasure in my virtue;
  give them constant cause to say,
    "Great is Yahweh,
  who likes to see his servant at peace!"

²⁸ Then my tongue will shout your goodness,
    and sing your praises all day long.

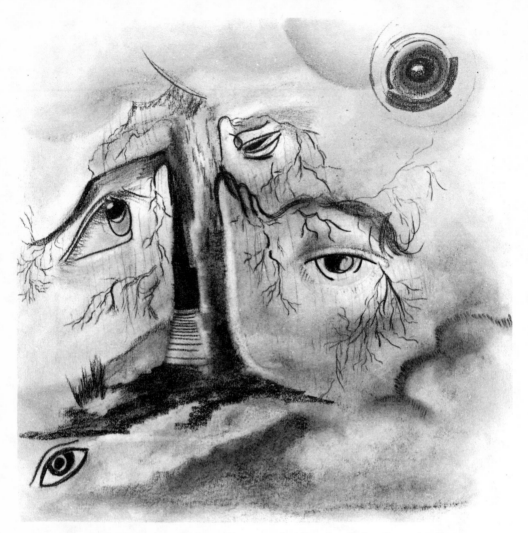

The wicked man's oracle is Sin / in the depths of his heart; / there is no fear of God / before his eyes.
(*Psalm 36:1*)

Psalm 36

For the choirmaster Of the servant of Yahweh, David

THE WICKEDNESS OF THE SINNER,
THE GOODNESS OF GOD

[1] The wicked man's oracle is Sin
    in the depths of his heart;
there is no fear of God
    before his eyes.

[2] He sees himself with too flattering an eye
to detect and detest his guilt;
[3] all he says tends to mischief and deceit,
    he has turned his back on wisdom.

[4] How best to work ·mischief he plots,
    even when he is in bed;
he persists in his evil course,
    he never rejects what is bad.

[5] Your love, Yahweh, reaches to the heavens,
your faithfulness to the clouds;
[6] your righteousness is like the mountains of God,
your judgments like the mighty deep.

Yahweh, protector of man and beast,
[7] how precious, God, your love!
Hence the sons of men
take shelter in the shadow of your wings.

[8] They feast on the bounty of your house,
you give them drink from your river of pleasure;
[9] yes, with you is the fountain of life,
by your light we see the light.

[10] Do not stop loving those who know you,
    or being righteous to upright hearts.
[11] Do not let arrogant feet crush me
    or wicked hands expel me.

[12] The evil men have fallen, there they lie,
beaten down, never to stand again!

Psalm 37

Of David

THE FATE OF THE VIRTUOUS AND THE WICKED

[1] Do not worry about the wicked,
do not envy those who do wrong.
[2] Quick as the grass they wither,
fading like the green in the field.

[3] Trust in Yahweh and do what is good,
make your home in the land and live in peace;
[4] make Yahweh your only joy
and he will give you what your heart desires.

[5] Commit your fate to Yahweh,
trust in him and he will act:
[6] making your virtue clear as the light,
your integrity as bright as noon.

[7] Be quiet before Yahweh, and wait patiently for him,
not worrying about men who make their fortunes,
about men who scheme
[14c] to bring the poor and needy down.

[8] Enough of anger, leave rage aside,
do not worry, nothing but evil can come of it:
[9] for the wicked will be expelled,
while those who hope in Yahweh shall have the land for their own.

[10] A little longer, and the wicked will be no more,
search his place well, he will not be there;
[11] but the humble shall have the land for their own
to enjoy untroubled peace.

[12] The wicked man plots against the virtuous,
and grinds his teeth at him;
[13] but the Lord only laughs at the man,
knowing his end is in sight.

[14a] Though the wicked draw the sword,
[14b] and bend their bow, to kill the upright,
[15] their swords will only pierce their own hearts
and their bows will be smashed.

[16] The little the virtuous possesses
outweighs all the wealth of the wicked,

Trust in Yahweh and do what is good, / make your home in the land and live in peace;
(Psalm 37:3)

[17] since the arms of the wicked are doomed to break,
and Yahweh will uphold the virtuous.

[18] Yahweh takes care of good men's lives,
and their heritage will last for ever;
[19] they will not be at a loss when bad times come,
in time of famine they will have more than they need.

[20] As for the wicked—they will perish,
these enemies of Yahweh;
they will vanish like the beauty of the meadows,
they will vanish in smoke.

[21] The wicked man borrows without meaning to repay,
but a virtuous man is generous and openhanded;
[22] those he blesses will have the land for their own,
those he curses will be expelled.

[23] Yahweh guides a man's steps,
they are sure, and he takes pleasure in his progress;
[24] he may fall, but never fatally,
since Yahweh supports him by the hand.

[25] Now I am old, but ever since my youth
I never saw a virtuous man deserted,
or his descendants forced to beg their bread;
[26] he is always compassionate, always lending:
his children will be blessed.

[27] Never yield to evil, practice good
and you will have an everlasting home,
[28] for Yahweh loves what is right,
and never deserts the devout.

Those who do wrong will perish once and for all,
and the children of the wicked shall be expelled;
[29] the virtuous will have the land for their own,
and make it their home for ever.

[30] The mouth of the virtuous man murmurs wisdom,
and his tongue speaks what is right;
[31] with the Law of his God in his heart
his steps can never falter.

[32] The wicked man spies on the virtuous,
seeking to kill him;
[33] Yahweh will never leave him in those clutches,
or let him be condemned under trial.

[34a] Put your hope in Yahweh, keep his way,
[40b] and he will save you from the wicked,
[34b] raising you until you make the land your own
and see the wicked expelled.

[35] I have seen the wicked in his triumph
towering like a cedar of Lebanon,
[36] but when next I passed, he was not there,
I looked for him and he was nowhere to be found.

[37] Observe the innocent man, consider the upright:
for the man of peace there are descendants,
[38] but sinners shall be destroyed altogether,
the descendants of the wicked shall be wiped out.

[39] The salvation of the virtuous comes from Yahweh,
he is their shelter when trouble comes;
[40a] Yahweh helps and rescues them,
he saves them because they take shelter in him.

Psalm 38

Psalm Of David In commemoration

PRAYER IN DISTRESS

[1] Yahweh, do not punish me in your rage,
or reprove me in the heat of anger.
[2] Your arrows have pierced deep,
your hand has pressed down on me;
[3] no soundness in my flesh now you are angry,
no health in my bones, because of my sin.

[4] My guilt is overwhelming me,
it is too heavy a burden;
[5] my wounds stink and are festering,
the result of my folly;
[6] bowed down, bent double, overcome,
I go mourning all the day.

[7] My loins are burned up with fever,
there is no soundness in my flesh:
[8] numbed and crushed and overcome,
my heart groans, I moan aloud.

[9] Lord, all that I long for is known to you,
my sighing is no secret from you;
[10] my heart is throbbing, my strength deserting me,
the light of my eyes itself has left me.

[11] My friends and my companions shrink from my wounds,
even the dearest of them keep their distance;
[12] men intent on killing me lay snares,
others, hoping to hurt me, threaten my ruin,
hatching treacherous plots all day.

[13] But I am like the deaf, I do not hear,
like the dumb man who does not open his mouth;
[14] I am like the man who, hearing nothing,
gives no sharp answer in return.

[15] For I put my trust in you, Yahweh,
and leave you to answer for me, Lord my God.
[16] I have already said, "Stop them gloating over me,
do not let them take advantage of me if my foot should slip."

[17] And now my fall is upon me,
there is no relief from my pains;

Your arrows have pierced deep, / your hand has pressed down on me;
(Psalm 38:2)

[18] yes, I admit my guilt,
   I am sorry for having sinned.

[19] There are more and more to hurt me for no reason,
   There are more to hate me unprovoked,
[20] repaying my kindness with evil,
   arraigning me for trying to do right.

[21] Yahweh, do not desert me,
   do not stand aside, my God!
[22] Come quickly to my help,
   Lord, my savior!

Psalm 39

For the choirmaster   For Jeduthun   Psalm   Of David

THE INSIGNIFICANCE OF MAN BEFORE GOD

¹ I said, "I will watch how I behave,
and not let my tongue lead me into sin;
I will keep a muzzle on my mouth
as long as the wicked man is near me."
² I stayed dumb, silent, speechless,
though the sight of him thriving made torment increase.

³ My heart had been smoldering inside me,
but it flared up at the thought of this
and the words burst out,
⁴ "Tell me, Yahweh, when my end will be,
how many days are allowed me,
show me how frail I am.

⁵ "Look, you have given me an inch or two of life,
my life-span is nothing to you;
each man that stands on earth is only a puff of wind,   *Pause*
⁶ every man that walks, only a shadow,
and the wealth he amasses is only a puff of wind—
he does not know who will take it next."

⁷ So tell me, Lord, what can I expect?
My hope is in you.
⁸ Free me from all my sins,
do not make me the butt of idiots.
⁹ I am dumb, I speak no more,
since you yourself have been at work.

¹⁰ Lay your scourge aside,
I am worn out with the blows you deal me.
¹¹ You punish man with the penalties of sin,
like a moth you eat away all that gives him pleasure—
man is indeed only a puff of wind!   *Pause*

¹² Yahweh, hear my prayer,
listen to my cry for help,
do not stay deaf to my crying.
I am your guest, and only for a time,
a nomad like all my ancestors.
¹³ Look away, let me draw breath,
before I go away and am no more!

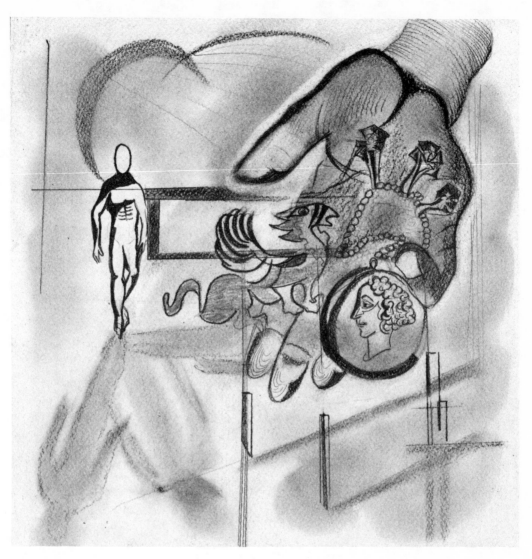

every man that walks, only a shadow, / and the wealth he amasses is only a puff of wind— / he does not know who will take it next."
(*Psalm 39:6*)

I waited and waited for Yahweh, / now at last he has stooped to me / and heard my cry for help.
(*Psalm 40:1*)

Psalm 40

For the choirmaster   Psalm   Of David

SONG OF PRAISE AND PRAYER FOR HELP

[1] I waited and waited for Yahweh,
  now at last he has stooped to me
  and heard my cry for help.

[2] He has pulled me out of the horrible pit,
  out of the slough of the marsh,
 has settled my feet on a rock
  and steadied my steps.

[3] He has put a new song in my mouth,
  a song of praise to our God;
 dread will seize many at the sight,
  and they will put their trust in Yahweh.

[4] Happy the man who puts
  his trust in Yahweh,
 and does not side with rebels
  who stray after false gods.

[5] How many wonders you have done for us,
  Yahweh, my God!
 How many plans you have made for us;
  you have no equal!
 I want to proclaim them, again and again,
  but they are more than I can count.

[6] You, who wanted no sacrifice or oblation,
  opened my ear,
 you asked no holocaust or sacrifice for sin;
[7]   then I said, "Here I am! I am coming!"

 In the scroll of the book am I not commanded
[8]   to obey your will?
 My God, I have always loved your Law
  from the depths of my being.

[9] I have always proclaimed the righteousness of Yahweh
  in the Great Assembly;
 nor do I mean to stop proclaiming,
  as you know well.

[10] I have never kept your righteousness to myself,
   but have spoken of your faithfulness and saving help;
I have made no secret of your love and faithfulness
   in the Great Assembly.

[11] For your part, Yahweh, do not withhold
   your kindness from me!
May your love and faithfulness
   constantly preserve me.

[12] More misfortunes beset me
   than I can count,
my sins close in on me
   until I can hardly see,
they outnumber the hairs on my head;
   my courage is running out.

[13] Oh come and rescue me, Yahweh,
Yahweh come quickly and help me!
[14] Shame and dishonor on all
who are out to kill, to destroy me!

   Down with them! Disgrace on those
      who enjoy my misfortune!
[15] May they be aghast with shame,
   those who say to me, "Aha! Aha!"

[16] But joy and gladness
   for all who seek you!
To all who love your saving power
   give constant cause to say, "God is great!"

[17] To me, poor wretch,
   come quickly, Lord!
My helper, my savior, my God,
   come and do not delay!

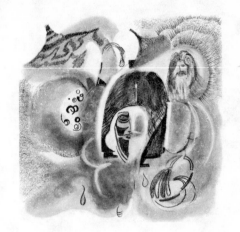

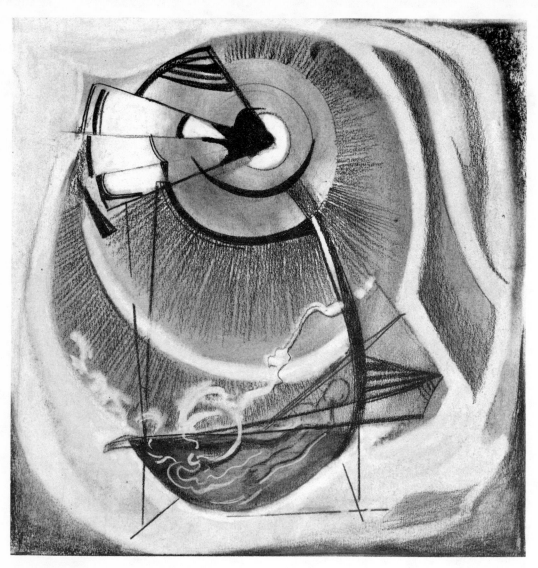

"*This sickness is fatal that has overtaken him, / he is down at last, he will never get up again.*"
(*Psalm 41:8*)

Psalm 41

For the choirmaster   Psalm   Of David

PRAYER OF A SICK AND LONELY MAN

[1] Happy the man who cares for the poor and the weak:
if disaster strikes, Yahweh will come to his help.
[2] Yahweh will guard him, give him life and happiness in the land;
ah, do not let his enemies treat him as they please!
[3] Yahweh will be his comfort on his bed of sickness;
most carefully you make his bed when he is sick.

[4] I for my part said, "Yahweh, take pity on me!
Cure me, for I have sinned against you."
[5] My enemies say of me with malice,
"How long before he dies and his name perishes?"
[6] They visit me, their hearts full of spite,
they offer hollow comfort, and go out to spread the news.

[7] All who hate me whisper to each other about me,
reckoning I deserve the misery I suffer,
[8] "This sickness is fatal that has overtaken him,
he is down at last, he will never get up again."
[9] Even my closest and most trusted friend,
who shared my table, rebels against me.

[10] But Yahweh, take pity on me!
Raise me up, and I will pay them back;
[11] and by this I shall know that I enjoy your favor,
if my enemy fails to triumph over me;
[12] and I, whom you uphold, go unscathed,
set by you in your presence for ever.

[13] Blessed be Yahweh, the God of Israel,
from all eternity and for ever!
Amen. Amen!

As a doe longs / for running streams, / so longs my soul / for you, my God.
(Psalm 42:1)

Psalm 42–43

For the choirmaster   Poem   Of the sons of Korah

LAMENT OF A LEVITE IN EXILE

¹ As a doe longs
   for running streams,
so longs my soul
   for you, my God.

² My soul thirsts for God,
   the God of life;
when shall I go to see
   the face of God?

³ I have no food but tears,
   day and night;
and all day long men say to me,
   "Where is your God?"

⁴ I remember, and my soul
   melts within me:
I am on my way to the wonderful Tent,
   to the house of God,
among cries of joy and praise
   and an exultant throng.

⁵ Why so downcast, my soul,
   why do you sigh within me?
Put your hope in God: I shall praise him yet,
⁶   my savior, ·my God.

When my soul is downcast within me,
   I think of you;
from the land of Jordan and of Hermon,
   of you, humble mountain!

⁷ Deep is calling to deep
   as your cataracts roar;
all your waves, your breakers,
   have rolled over me.

⁸ In the daytime may Yahweh
   command his love to come,
and by night may his song be on my lips,
   a prayer to the God of my life!

[9] Let me say to God my Rock,
    "Why do you forget me?
Why must I walk
    so mournfully, oppressed by the enemy?"

[10] Nearly breaking my bones
    my oppressors insult me,
as all day long they ask me,
    "Where is your God?"

[11] Why so downcast, my soul,
    why do you sigh within me?
Put your hope in God: I shall praise him yet,
    my savior, my God.

43

[1] Defend me, take up my cause
    against people who have no pity;
from the treacherous and cunning man
    rescue me, God.

[2] It is you, God, who are my shelter:
    why do you abandon me?
Why must I walk
    so mournfully, oppressed by the enemy?

[3] Send out your light and your truth,
    let these be my guide,
to lead me to your holy mountain
    and to the place where you live.

[4] Then I shall go to the altar of God,
    to the God of my joy,
I shall rejoice, I shall praise you on the harp,
    Yahweh, my God.

[5] Why so downcast, my soul,
    why do you sigh within me?
Put your hope in God: I shall praise him yet,
    my savior, my God.

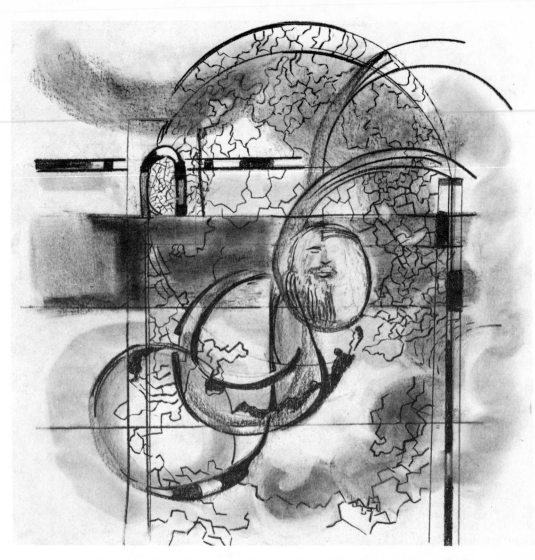

Then I shall go to the altar of God, / to the God of my joy, / I shall rejoice, I shall praise you on the harp, / Yahweh, my God.
(*Psalm* 43:4)

No, *it* is for your sake we are being massacred daily, / and counted as sheep for the slaughter.
(*Psalm* 44:22)

Psalm 44

For the choirmaster   Of the sons of Korah   Psalm

NATIONAL LAMENT

¹ God, we have heard with our own ears,
  our ancestors have told us
  of the deeds you performed in their days,
² in days long ago, ·by your hand.

  To put them in the land you dispossessed the nations,
  you harried the peoples to make room for them;
³ it was not by their swords they won the land,
  it was not by their arms they gained the victory:
  it was your right hand, your arm
  and the light of your face—because you loved them.

⁴ You it was, my King, my God,
  who won those victories for Jacob;
⁵ through you we trampled down our enemies
  through your name we subdued our aggressors.

⁶ My trust was not in my bow,
  my sword did not gain me victory;
⁷ we conquered our enemies through you,
  you, who defeated all who hated us—
⁸ our boast was always of God,
  we praised your name without ceasing.   *Pause*

⁹ Yet now you abandon and scorn us,
  you no longer march with our armies,
¹⁰ you allow the enemy to push us back,
  and let those who hate us raid us when it suits them.

¹¹ You let us go to the slaughterhouse like sheep,
  you scatter us among the nations;
¹² you sell your people for next to nothing,
  and make no profit from the bargain.

¹³ Thanks to you, our neighbors insult us,
  all those around us make us their butt and laughingstock;
¹⁴ you make us a byword to pagans,
  a thing to make them toss their heathen heads.

¹⁵ All day long I brood on this disgrace,
  my face covered in shame,

[16] under a shower of insult and blasphemy,
a display of hatred and revenge.

[17] All this happened to us though we had not forgotten you,
though we had not been disloyal to your covenant;
[18] though our hearts had not turned away,
though our steps had not left your path:
[19] yet you crushed us in the place where the jackals live,
and threw the shadow of death over us.

[20] Had we forgotten the name of our own God
and stretched out our hands to a foreign one,
[21] would not God have found this out,
he who knows the secrets of the heart?
[22] No, it is for your sake we are being massacred daily,
and counted as sheep for the slaughter.

[23] Wake up, Lord! Why are you asleep?
Awake! Do not abandon us for good.
[24] Why do you hide your face,
and forget we are wretched and exploited?

[25] For we are bowed in the dust,
our bodies crushed to the ground,
[26] Rise! Come to our help!
Redeem us for the sake of your love.

Psalm 45

For the choirmaster Tune: "Lilies . . ." Of the sons of Korah
Poem Love song

ROYAL WEDDING SONG

[1] My heart is stirred by a noble theme:
I address my poem to the king;
my tongue as ready as the pen of a busy scribe.

[2] Of all men you are the most handsome,
your lips are moist with grace,
for God has blessed you for ever.

[3] Hero, strap your sword at your side,
[4] in majesty and splendor; ·on, ride on,
in the cause of truth, religion and virtue!

Stretch the bowstring tight,
lending terror to your right hand.
[5] Your arrows are sharp; nations lie at your mercy,
the king's enemies are losing heart.

[6] Your throne, God, shall last for ever and ever,
your royal scepter is a scepter of integrity:
[7] virtue you love as much as you hate wickedness.

This is why God, your God, has anointed you
with the oil of gladness, above all your rivals;
[8] myrrh and aloes waft from your robes.

From palaces of ivory harps entertain you,
[9] daughters of kings are among your maids of honor;
on your right stands the queen, in gold from Ophir.

[10] Listen, daughter, pay careful attention:
forget your nation and your ancestral home,
[11] then the king will fall in love with your beauty.
He is your master now, bow down to him.

[12] The daughter of Tyre will solicit your favor with gifts,
[13] the wealthiest nations, ·with jewels set in gold.

[14] Dressed ·in brocades, the king's daughter
is led in to the king, with bridesmaids in her train.

Her ladies-in-waiting follow
[15] and enter the king's palace to general rejoicing.

in majesty and splendor; on, ride on, / in the cause of truth, religion and virtue!
(*Psalm 45:4*)

[16] Your ancestors will be replaced by sons
   whom you will make lords of the whole world.

[17] I shall immortalize your name,
   nations will sing your praises for ever and ever.

and its waters roar and seethe, / the mountains tottering as it heaves.
(*Psalm 46:3*)

Psalm 46

For the choirmaster   Of the sons of Korah   For oboe   Song

GOD IS ON OUR SIDE

[1] God is our shelter, our strength,
   ever ready to help in time of trouble,
[2] so we shall not be afraid when the earth gives way,
   when mountains tumble into the depths of the sea,
[3] and its waters roar and seethe,
   the mountains tottering as it heaves.

   (Yahweh Sabaoth is on our side,
      our citadel, the God of Jacob!)   *Pause*

[4] There is a river whose streams refresh the city of God,
   and it sanctifies the dwelling of the Most High.
[5] God is inside the city, she can never fall,
   at crack of dawn God helps her;
[6] to the roaring of nations and tottering of kingdoms,
   when he shouts, the world disintegrates.

[7]   Yahweh Sabaoth is on our side,
      our citadel, the God of Jacob!   *Pause*

[8] Come, think of Yahweh's marvels,
   the astounding things he has done in the world;
[9] all over the world he puts an end to wars,
   he breaks the bow, he snaps the spear,
   he gives shields to the flames.
[10] "Pause a while and know that I am God,
   exalted among the nations, exalted over the earth!"

[11]   Yahweh Sabaoth is on our side,
      our citadel, the God of Jacob!   *Pause*

117

God is king of the whole world: / play your best in his honor!
(*Psalm 47:7*)

Psalm 47

For the choirmaster   Of the sons of Korah   Psalm

YAHWEH, KING OF ISRAEL, LORD OF THE WORLD

[1] Clap your hands, all you peoples,
acclaim God with shouts of joy;
[2] for Yahweh, the Most High, is to be dreaded,
the Great King of the whole world.

[3] He brings the peoples under our dominion,
he puts the nations under our feet;
[4] for us he chooses our heritage—
the pride of Jacob, whom he loved.

[5] God rises to shouts of acclamation,
Yahweh rises to a blast of trumpets,
[6] let the music sound for our God, let it sound,
let the music sound for our King, let it sound!

[7] God is king of the whole world:
play your best in his honor!
[8] God is king of the nations,
he reigns on his holy throne.

[9] The leaders of the nations rally
to the people of the God of Abraham.
Every shield in the world belongs to God.
He reigns supreme.

Yahweh is great and supremely to be praised / in the city of our God,
(*Psalm 48:1*)

Psalm 48

Song   Psalm   Of the sons of Korah

ZION, THE MOUNTAIN OF GOD

¹ Yahweh is great and supremely to be praised
    in the city of our God,
² the holy mountain, ·beautiful where it rises,
    joy of the whole world;

Mount of Zion, deep heart of the North,
    city of the Great King;
³ here among her palaces,
    God proved to be her fortress.

⁴ There was a rallying, once, of kings,
    advancing together along a common front;
⁵ they looked, they were amazed,
    they panicked, they ran!

⁶ There they shuddered and writhed
    like women in labor,
⁷ it was the east wind, that wrecker
    of ships of Tarshish!

⁸ What we had heard we saw for ourselves
    in the city of our God,
the city of Yahweh Sabaoth,
    God-protected for ever.   *Pause*

⁹ God, in your Temple
    we reflect on your love:
¹⁰ God, your praise, like your name,
    reaches to the ends of the world.

Your right hand holds the victory;
¹¹   Mount Zion rejoices,
the daughters of Judah exult
    to have your rulings.

¹² Go through Zion, walk around her,
    counting her towers,
¹³ admiring her walls,
    reviewing her palaces;

then tell the next generation
¹⁴   that God is here,
our God and leader,
    for ever and ever.

Psalm 49

For the choirmaster   Of the sons of Korah   Psalm

THE FUTILITY OF RICHES

¹ Hear this, all nations,
  pay attention all who live on earth,
² important people, ordinary people,
  rich and poor alike!

³ My lips have wisdom to utter,
  my heart whispers sound sense;
⁴ I turn my attention to a proverb,
  and set my solution to the harp.

⁵ Why should I be afraid in evil times,
  when malice dogs my steps and hems me in,
⁶ of men who trust in their wealth
  and boast of the profusion of their riches?

⁷ But man could never redeem himself
  or pay his ransom to God:
⁸ it costs so much to redeem his life,
⁹ it is beyond him; ·how then could he live on for ever
  and never see the Pit—

¹⁰ when all the time he sees that wise men die;
  that foolish and stupid perish both alike,
  and leave their fortunes to others.

¹¹ Their tombs are their eternal home,
  their lasting residence,
  though they owned estates that bore their names.

¹² Man when he prospers forfeits intelligence:
  he is one with the cattle doomed to slaughter.
¹³ So on they go with their self-assurance,
  with men to run after them when they raise their voice.   *Pause*

¹⁴ Like sheep to be penned in Sheol,
  Death will herd them to pasture
  and the upright will have the better of them.

  Dawn will come and then the show they made will disappear,
  Sheol the home for them!
¹⁵ But God will redeem my life
  from the grasp of Sheol and will receive me.   *Pause*

Do not be afraid when a man grows rich, / when the glory of his House increases;
(Psalm 49:16)

¹⁶ Do not be afraid when a man grows rich,
  when the glory of his House increases;
¹⁷ when he dies he can take nothing with him,
  his glory cannot follow him down.

¹⁸ The soul he made so happy while he lived
  —"look after yourself and men will praise you"—
¹⁹ will join the company of his ancestors
  who will never see the light of day again.

²⁰ Man in his prosperity forfeits intelligence:
  he is one with the cattle doomed to slaughter.

I know all the birds of the air, / nothing moves in the field that does not belong to me.
(*Psalm 50:11*)

Psalm 50

Psalm Of Asaph

WORSHIP IN SPIRIT AND TRUTH

[1] Yahweh, God of Gods,
speaks, he summons the earth.
From east to west,
[2] from Zion, perfection of beauty, he shines.
[3] Let our God come, and be silent no more!

Preceding him, a devouring fire,
around him, a raging storm;
[4] he summons the heavens above
and the earth, to his people's trial:

[5] "Assemble my faithful before me
who sealed my covenant by sacrifice!"
[6] Let the heavens proclaim his righteousness
when God himself is judge!

[7a] "Listen, my people, I am speaking;
[7b] Israel, I am giving evidence against you!
[21c] I charge, I indict you to your face,
[7c] I, God, your God.

[8] "I am not finding fault with your sacrifices,
those holocausts constantly before me;
[9] I do not claim one extra bull from your homes,
nor one extra goat from your pens,

[10] "since all the forest animals are already mine,
and the cattle on my mountains in their thousands;
[11] I know all the birds of the air,
nothing moves in the field that does not belong to me.

[12] "If I were hungry, I should not tell you,
since the world and all it holds is mine.
[13] Do I eat the flesh of bulls,
or drink goats' blood?

[14] "No, let thanksgiving be your sacrifice to God,
fulfill the vows you make to the Most High;
[15] then you can invoke me in your troubles
and I will rescue you, and you shall honor me."

[16] But to the wicked man God says:

"What business have you reciting my statutes,
  standing there mouthing my covenant,
¹⁷ since you detest my discipline
  and thrust my words behind you?

¹⁸ "You make friends with a thief as soon as you see one,
  you feel at home with adulterers,
¹⁹ your mouth is given freely to evil
  and your tongue to inventing lies.

²⁰ "You sit there, slandering your own brother,
  you malign your own mother's son.
²¹ You do this, and expect me to say nothing?
²¹ᵇ Do you really think I am like you?

²² "You are leaving God out of account; take care!
  Or I will tear you to pieces where no one can rescue you!
²³ Whoever makes thanksgiving his sacrifice honors me;
  to the upright man I will show how God can save."

Psalm 51

*For the choirmaster Psalm Of David When the prophet Nathan
came to him because he had been with Bathsheba*

MISERERE

1 Have mercy on me, O God, in your goodness,
in your great tenderness wipe away my faults;
2 wash me clean of my guilt,
purify me from my sin.

3 For I am well aware of my faults,
I have my sin constantly in mind,
4 having sinned against none other than you,
having done what you regard as wrong.

You are just when you pass sentence on me,
blameless when you give judgment.
5 You know I was born guilty,
a sinner from the moment of conception.

6 Yet, since you love sincerity of heart,
teach me the secrets of wisdom.
7 Purify me with hyssop until I am clean;
wash me until I am whiter than snow.

8 Instill some joy and gladness into me,
let the bones you have crushed rejoice again.
9 Hide your face from my sins,
wipe out all my guilt.

10 God, create a clean heart in me,
put into me a new and constant spirit,
11 do not banish me from your presence,
do not deprive me of your holy spirit.

12 Be my savior again, renew my joy,
keep my spirit steady and willing;
13 and I shall teach transgressors the way to you,
and to you the sinners will return.

14 Save me from death, God my savior,
and my tongue will acclaim your righteousness;
15 Lord, open my lips,
and my mouth will speak out your praise.

Then there will be proper sacrifice to please you / —holocaust and whole oblation— / and young bulls to be offered on your altar.
(*Psalm 51:19*)

[16] Sacrifice gives you no pleasure,
were I to offer holocaust, you would not have it.
[17] My sacrifice is this broken spirit,
you will not scorn this crushed and broken heart.

[18] Show your favor graciously to Zion.
rebuild the walls of Jerusalem.
[19] Then there will be proper sacrifice to please you
—holocaust and whole oblation—
and young bulls to be offered on your altar.

That is why God will crush you, / snatch you away for good, / tear you out of your tent, / uproot you from the land of the living.
(Psalm 52:5)

Psalm 52

*For the choirmaster Poem Of David When Doeg the Edomite went
and warned Saul, "David has gone to Ahimelech's house"*

THE FATE OF CYNICS

¹ Why make a boast of your wickedness,
    you champion in villainy,
² all day ·plotting destruction?
  Your tongue is razor sharp,
    you artist in perfidy!

³ You prefer evil to good,
    lying to honest speech;   *Pause*
⁴ you love the destructive word,
    perfidious tongue!

⁵ That is why God will crush you,
    snatch you away for good,
    tear you out of your tent,
  uproot you from the land of the living.   *Pause*

⁶ Dread will seize the virtuous at the sight,
    they will laugh at his fate:
⁷ "So much for the man who refused
    to make God his fortress,
  but relied on his own great wealth
    and drew his strength from crime!"

⁸ I, for my part, like an olive tree
    growing in the house of God,
  put my trust in God's love
    for ever and ever.

⁹ I mean to thank you constantly
    for doing what you did,
  and put my hope in your name, that is so full of kindness,
    in the presence of those who love you.

All have turned aside, / all alike are tainted / There is not one good man left, / not a single one.
(*Psalm* 53:3)

Psalm 53

For the choirmaster   In sickness   Poem   Of David

THE GODLESS MAN

[1] The fool says in his heart,
   "There is no God!"
They are false, corrupt, vile,
   there is not one good man left.

[2] God is looking down from heaven
   at the sons of men,
to see if a single one is wise,
   if a single one is seeking God.

[3] All have turned aside,
   all alike are tainted
There is not one good man left,
   not a single one.

[4] Are they so ignorant, these evil men
   who swallow my people
as though they were eating bread,
   and never invoke God?

[5] They will be struck with fear,
   fear without reason,
since God scatters the bones of the apostate,
   they are disgraced, for God rejects them.

[6] Who will bring Israel salvation from Zion?
When God brings his people home,
   what joy for Jacob, what happiness for Israel!

But now God himself comes to help me, / the Lord, supporter of my life.
(*Psalm* 54:4)

Psalm 54

For the choirmaster   On stringed instruments   Poem   Of David   When the Ziphites went to Saul and said, "Is not David hiding with us?"

AN APPEAL TO THE GOD OF JUSTICE

[1] God, save me by your name,
   by your power see justice done to me;
[2] God, hear my prayer,
   listen to what I am saying!

[3] Arrogant men are attacking me,
   brutes who are hounding me to death,
   people to whom God means nothing.   *Pause*

[4] But now God himself comes to help me,
   the Lord, supporter of my life.
[5] May their wickedness recoil on themselves,
   Yahweh, ever faithful, destroy my enemies!

[6] How gladly will I offer sacrifice to you
   and praise your name, that is so full of kindness.
[7] He has rescued me from all my troubles,
   and let me see my enemies defeated.

And I say, / "Oh for the wings of a dove / to fly away and find rest."
(*Psalm 55:6*)

Psalm 55

For the choirmaster For strings Poem Of David

PRAYER IN PERSECUTION

[1] God, hear my prayer,
  do not hide from my petition,
[2] give me a hearing, answer me,
  I cannot rest for complaining.

[3] I shudder ·at the enemy's shouts,
  at the howling of the wicked;
they bring misery crashing down on me,
  and vent their fury on me.

[4] My heart aches in my breast,
Death's terrors assail me,
[5] fear and trembling descend on me,
  horror overwhelms me.

[6] And I say,
  "Oh for the wings of a dove
    to fly away and find rest."
[7] How far I would take my flight,
  and make a new home in the desert! *Pause*

[8] There I should soon find shelter
  from the raging wind,
[9] and from the tempest, ·Lord, that destroys,
  and from their malicious tongues.

I can see how Violence
  and Discord fill the city;
[10] day and night they stalk together
  along the city walls.

Sorrow and Misery live inside,
[11]   Ruin is an inmate;
Tyranny and Treachery are never absent
  from its central square.

[12] Were it an enemy who insulted me,
  I could put up with that;
had a rival got the better of me,
  I could hide from him.

¹³ But you, a man of my own rank,
　　a colleague and a friend,
¹⁴ to whom sweet conversation bound me
　　in the house of God!

　　May they recoil in disorder,
¹⁵ may Death descend on them,
　may they go down, still living, to Sheol—
　since Evil shares their homes.

¹⁶ I, for myself, appeal to God
　　and Yahweh saves me;
¹⁷ evening, morning, noon,
　　I complain, I groan;
　　he will hear me calling.

¹⁸ His peace can ransom me
　　from the war being waged on me.
　How many are ranged against me!
¹⁹ 　But God will hear me.

　Sovereign from the first, he will humble them;　 *Pause*

　no change of heart for them,
　　since they do not fear God.

²⁰ He has attacked his friends,
　　he has gone back on his word;
²¹ though his mouth is smoother than butter,
　　he has war in his heart;
　his words may soothe more than oil,
　　but they are naked swords.

²² Unload your burden on to Yahweh,
　　and he will support you;
　he will never permit
　　the virtuous to falter.

²³ As for these murderous, these treacherous men,
　　you, God, will push them
　down to the deepest Pit
　　before half their days are out.

　For my part, I put my trust in you.

for you have rescued me from Death / to walk in the presence of
God / in the light of the living.
(*Psalm 56:13*)

Psalm 56

For the choirmaster Tune: "Dove of the distant gods" Of David Miktam When the Philistines held him in Gath

RELIANCE ON GOD

[1] Take pity on me, God, as they harry me,
  pressing their attacks home all day.
[2] All day my opponents harry me,
  hordes coming in to the attack.

[3] Raise me up ·when I am most afraid,
  I put my trust in you;
[4] in God, whose word I praise,
  in God I put my trust, fearing nothing;
  what can men do to me?

[5] All day long they twist what I say,
  all they think of is how to harm me,
[6] they conspire, lurk, spy on my movements,
  determined to take my life.

[7] Are they to go unpunished for such a crime?
  God, in fury bring the nations down!
[8] You have noted my agitation,
  now collect my tears in your wineskin!
[9] Then my enemies will have to fall back
    as soon as I call for help.

  This I know: that God is on my side.
[10] In God whose word I praise,
  in Yahweh, whose word I praise,
[11] in God I put my trust, fearing nothing;
  what can man do to me?

[12] I must fulfill the vows I made you, God;
  I shall pay you my thank offerings,
[13] for you have rescued me from Death
  to walk in the presence of God
    in the light of the living.

Rise high above the heavens, God, / let your glory be over the earth!
(*Psalm* 57:5)

Psalm 57

*For the choirmaster Tune: "Do not destroy" Of David Miktam
When he escaped from Saul, in the cave*

AMONG FEROCIOUS ENEMIES

[1] Take pity on me, God, take pity on me,
in you my soul takes shelter;
I take shelter in the shadow of your wings
until the destroying storm is over.

[2] I call on God the Most High,
on God who has done everything for me:
[3] to send from heaven and save me,
to check the people harrying me,   *Pause*
may God send his faithfulness and love.

[4] I lie surrounded by lions
greedy for human prey,
their teeth are spears and arrows,
their tongue a sharp sword.

[5] Rise high above the heavens, God,
let your glory be over the earth!
[6] They laid a net where I was walking
when I was bowed with care;
they dug a pitfall for me
but fell into it themselves!   *Pause*

[7] My heart is ready, God,
my heart is ready;
I mean to sing and play for you,
[8]   awake, my muse,
awake, lyre and harp,
I mean to wake the Dawn!

[9] Lord, I mean to thank you among the peoples,
to play music to you among the nations;
[10] your love is high as heaven,
your faithfulness as the clouds.
[11] Rise high above the heavens, God,
let your glory be over the earth!

like a slug that melts as it moves, / like an abortion, denied the light of day!
(*Psalm* 58:8)

Psalm 58

For the choirmaster   Tune: "Do not destroy"   Of David   Miktam

THE JUDGE OF EARTHLY JUDGES

[1] Gods you may be, but do you give the sentences you should,
and dispense impartial justice to mankind?
[2] On the contrary, in your hearts you meditate oppression,
with your hands you dole out tyranny on earth.

[3]   Right from the womb these wicked men have gone astray,
these double talkers have been in error since their birth;
[4] their poison is the poison of the snake,
they are deaf as the adder that blocks its ears
[5] so as not to hear the magician's music
and the clever snake charmer's spells.

[6] God, break their teeth in their mouths,
Yahweh, wrench out the fangs of these savage lions!
[7] May they drain away like water running to waste,
may they wither like trodden grass,
[8] like a slug that melts as it moves,
like an abortion, denied the light of day!

[9] Before they sprout thorns like the bramble,
green or scorched, may the wrath whirl them away!
[10] What joy for the virtuous, seeing this vengeance,
bathing their feet in the blood of the wicked!
[11] "So," people will say, "the virtuous do have their harvest;
so there is a God who dispenses justice on earth!"

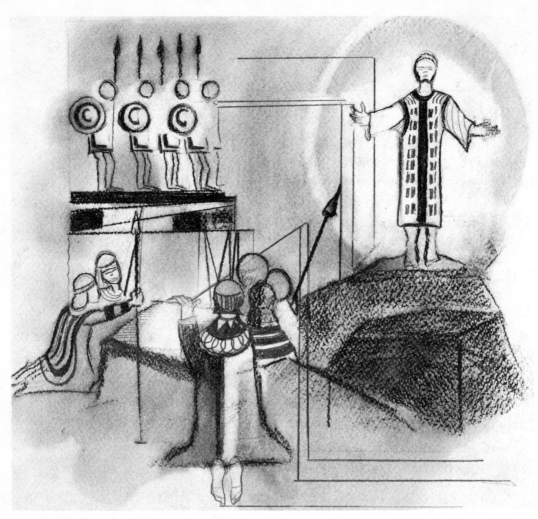

Rescue me from my enemies, my God, / protect me from those attacking me,
(*Psalm 59:1*)

Psalm 59

*For the choirmaster Tune: "Do not destroy" Of David Miktam
When Saul sent spies to his house to have him killed*

AGAINST THE WICKED

[1] Rescue me from my enemies, my God,
 protect me from those attacking me,
[2] rescue me from these evil men,
 save me from these murderers!

[3] Look at them lurking to ambush me,
 they are strong and united against me;
[4] for no fault, no sin, ·no offense of mine,
 Yahweh, how they hurry into position!

 Wake up, stand by me and look,
[5] Yahweh, God of Sabaoth, God of Israel,
 up, now, and punish these pagans,
 show no mercy to these villains and traitors! *Pause*

[6] Back they come at nightfall,
  snarling like curs,
  prowling through the town.

[7] See how they slaver at the mouth,
 with swords between their teeth,
 "There is no one listening."

[8] Yahweh, you laugh at them,
 you make fun of these pagans.
[9] My Strength, I look to you.

 My citadel is God himself,
[10] the God who loves me is coming,
 God will show me my enemies defeated.

[11] Slaughter them, God, before my people forget!
 Harry them with your power and strike them down,
  Lord, our shield!

[12] Sin is in their mouths, sin on their lips,
 so let them be caught in their pride!
 For the curses and lies they utter,

[13] destroy them in anger, destroy, until they are finished,
 until God is acknowledged as ruler in Jacob
 to the remotest parts of the earth! *Pause*

147

¹⁴ Back they come at nightfall,
   snarling like curs,
   prowling through the town;
¹⁵ scavenging for food,
   growling till they are full.

¹⁶ I, for my part, celebrate your strength,
   I sing of your love morning by morning;
   you have always been my citadel,
   a shelter when I am in trouble.

¹⁷ My Strength, I play for you,
   my citadel is God himself,
      the God who loves me.

You have made the earth tremble, torn it apart; / now mend the rifts, it is tottering still!
(*Psalm 60:2*)

Psalm 60

*For the choirmaster Tune: "The decree is a lily" Miktam Of David
For instruction When he was at war with Aram-naharaim and Aram-
zobah, and Joab marched back to destroy twelve thousand Edomites
in the Valley of Salt*

NATIONAL PRAYER AFTER DEFEAT

1 God, you have rejected us, broken us;
  you have been angry, come back to us!

2 You have made the earth tremble, torn it apart;
  now mend the rifts, it is tottering still!
3 You have allowed your people to suffer,
  to drink a wine that makes us reel.

4 Hoist the standard to rally those who fear you,
  to put them out of range of bow and arrow. *Pause*

5 To bring rescue to those you love,
  save with your right hand and answer us!

6 God promised us once from his sanctuary,
  "I the Victor will parcel out Shechem,
  and share out the Valley of Succoth.

7 "Gilead is mine, Manasseh mine,
  Ephraim is my helmet,
  Judah, my marshal's baton.

8 "Moab a bowl for me to wash in!
  I throw my sandal over Edom.
  Now shout 'Victory' Philistia!"

9 Who is there now to take me into the fortified city,
  to lead me into Edom?
10 God, can you really have rejected us?
  You no longer march with our armies.

11 Help us in this hour of crisis,
  the help that man can give is worthless.
12 With God among us we shall fight like heroes,
  he will trample on our enemies.

From the end of the earth I call to you, / with sinking heart.
(*Psalm 61:2*)

Psalm 61

For the choirmaster   For strings   Of David

PRAYER OF AN EXILE

[1] God, hear my cry for help,
   listen to my prayer!
[2] From the end of the earth I call to you,
   with sinking heart.

  To the rock too high for me,
   lead me!
[3] For you are my refuge,
   a strong tower against the enemy.

[4] Let me stay in your tent for ever,
   taking refuge in the shelter of your wings.   *Pause*
[5] You, God, accept my vows,
   you grant me the heritage of those who fear your name.

[6]   Let the king live on and on,
   prolong his years, generation on generation.
[7] May he sit enthroned in God's presence for ever!
   Assign your Love and Faithfulness to guard him!

[8] So I shall always sing of your name,
   fulfilling the vows I have taken, day after day.

Rest in God alone, my soul! / He is the source of my hope;
(*Psalm 62:5*)

Psalm 62

For the choirmaster . . . Jeduthun   Psalm   Of David

HOPE IN GOD ALONE

[1] In God alone there is rest for my soul,
    from him comes my safety;
[2] with him alone for my rock, my safety,
    my fortress, I can never fall.

[3] How many times will you come rushing at a man,
    all of you, to bring him down
like a wall already leaning over,
    like a rampart undermined?

[4] Deceit their sole intention,
    their delight is to mislead;
with lies on their lips they bless aloud,
    while cursing inwardly.   *Pause*

[5] Rest in God alone, my soul!
    He is the source of my hope;
[6] with him alone for my rock, my safety,
    my fortress, I can never fall;
[7] rest in God, my safety, my glory,
    the rock of my strength.

[8] In God, I find shelter; ·rely on him
    people, at all times;
unburden your hearts to him,
    God is a shelter for us.   *Pause*

[9] Ordinary men are only a puff of wind,
    important men delusion;
put both in the scales and up they go,
    lighter than a puff of wind.
[10] Put no reliance on extortion,
    no empty hopes in robbery;
though riches may increase,
    keep your heart detached.
[11] God has spoken once,
    twice I have heard this:
it is for God to be strong,
[12]   for you, Lord, to be loving;
and you yourself repay
    man as his works deserve.

God, you are my God, I am seeking you, / my soul is thirsting for
you, / my flesh is longing for you, / a land parched, weary and waterless;
(Psalm 63:1)

Psalm 63

Psalm Of David   When he was in the wilderness of Judah

DESIRE FOR GOD

[1] God, you are my God, I am seeking you,
   my soul is thirsting for you,
   my flesh is longing for you,
   a land parched, weary and waterless;
[2] I long to gaze on you in the Sanctuary,
   and to see your power and glory.

[3] Your love is better than life itself,
   my lips will recite your praise;
[4] all my life I will bless you,
   in your name lift up my hands;
[5] my soul will feast most richly,
   on my lips a song of joy and, in my mouth, praise.

[6] On my bed I think of you,
   I meditate on you all night long,
[7] for you have always helped me.
   I sing for joy in the shadow of your wings;
[8] my soul clings close to you,
   your right hand supports me.

[9] But may those now hounding me to death
   go down to the earth below,
[10] consigned to the edge of the sword,
   and left as food for jackals.
[11] Then will the king rejoice in God,
   and all who swear by him be able to boast
   once these lying mouths are silenced.

*God will shoot them with his own arrow, / wound them without warn-
ing.*
(*Psalm 64:7*)

Psalm 64

For the choirmaster   Psalm   Of David

THE PUNISHMENT FOR SLANDERERS

¹ God, hear me as I make my plea,
  protect me from this frightening enemy,
² hide me from the wicked and their schemes,
  from this mob of evil men,

³ sharpening their tongues like swords,
  shooting bitter words like arrows,
⁴ shooting them at the innocent from cover,
  shooting suddenly, without warning.

⁵ Urging each other on to their wicked purpose,
  they discuss where to hide their snares.
  "Who is going to see us?" they say,
⁶   "Who can probe our secrets?"
  Who? He who probes the inmost mind
    and the depths of the heart.

⁷ God will shoot them with his own arrow,
  wound them without warning.
⁸ He will destroy them for that tongue of theirs,
  and all who see them fall will shake their heads.

⁹   Then all will feel afraid,
  will tell others what God has done;
    they will understand why he has done it.
¹⁰ The virtuous will rejoice in Yahweh,
    will make him their refuge;
  and upright hearts will be able to boast.

Psalm 65

For the choirmaster   Of David   Song

THANKSGIVING HYMN

¹ Praise is rightfully yours,
   God, in Zion.
Vows to you must be fulfilled,
²   for you answer prayer.

All flesh must come to you
³   with all its sins;
though our faults overpower us,
   you blot them out.

⁴ Happy the man you choose, whom you invite
   to live in your courts.
Fill us with the good things of your house,
   of your holy Temple.

⁵ Your righteousness repays us with marvels,
   God our savior,
hope of all the ends of the earth
   and the distant islands.

⁶ Your strength holds the mountains up,
   such is the power that wraps you;
⁷ you calm the clamor of the ocean,
   the clamor of its waves.

⁸ The nations are in uproar, ·in panic
   those who live at the ends of the world,
as your miracles bring shouts of joy
   to the portals of morning and evening.

⁹ You visit the earth and water it,
   you load it with riches;
God's rivers brim with water
   to provide their grain.

¹⁰   This is how you provide it:
   by drenching its furrows, by leveling its ridges,
   by softening it with showers, by blessing the first fruits.
¹¹ You crown the year with your bounty,
   abundance flows wherever you pass;

the meadows are dressed in flocks, / the valleys are clothed in wheat, / what shouts of joy, what singing!
(Psalm 65:13)

¹² the desert pastures overflow,
  the hillsides are wrapped in joy,
¹³ the meadows are dressed in flocks,
  the valleys are clothed in wheat,
  what shouts of joy, what singing!

Psalm 66

For the choirmaster Song Psalm

CORPORATE ACT OF THANKSGIVING

¹ Acclaim God, all the earth,
² play music to the glory of his name,
  glorify him with your praises,
³ say to God, "What dread you inspire!"

  Your achievements are the measure of your power.
  Your enemies cringe in your presence;
⁴ all the earth bows down to you,
  playing music for you, playing in honor of your name. *Pause*

⁵ Come and see what marvels God has done,
  so much to be feared for his deeds among mankind:
⁶ he turned the sea into dry land,
  they crossed the river on foot!

  So let us rejoice in him,
⁷ who rules for ever by his power:
  his eyes keep watch on the nations,
  let no rebel raise his head! *Pause*

⁸ You nations, bless our God
  and make his praise resound,
⁹ who brings our soul to life
  and keeps our feet from faltering.

¹⁰ You tested us, God,
  you refined us like silver,
¹¹ you let us fall into the net,
  you laid heavy burdens on our backs,
¹² you let people drive over our heads;
  but now the ordeal by fire and water is over,
  and you allow us once more to draw breath.

¹³ I bring holocausts to your house,
  I bring them to fulfill those vows
¹⁴ that rose to my lips,
  those vows I spoke when in trouble.

¹⁵ I offer you fat holocausts
  and the smoke of burning rams,
  I offer you bullocks and he-goats. *Pause*

Acclaim God, all the earth,
(*Psalm 66:1*)

16 Come and listen, all you who fear God,
  while I tell you what he has done for me:
17 when I uttered my cry to him
  and high praise was on my tongue,
18 had I been guilty in my heart,
  the Lord would never have heard me.
19 But God not only heard me,
  he listened to my prayer.

20   Blessed be God,
  who neither ignored my prayer
  nor deprived me of his love.

Let the nations praise you, God, / Let all the nations praise you!
(*Psalm 67:5*)

Psalm 67

For the choirmaster   For strings   Psalm   Song

HARVEST SONG

[1] May God show kindness and bless us,
   and make his face smile on us!   *Pause*
[2] For then the earth will acknowledge your ways
   and all the nations will know of your power to save.

[3] Let the nations praise you, O God,
   let all the nations praise you!

[4] Let the nations shout and sing for joy,
   since you dispense true justice to the world;
   you dispense strict justice to the peoples,
   on earth you rule the nations.   *Pause*

[5] Let the nations praise you, God,
   Let all the nations praise you!

[6] The soil has given its harvest,
   God, our God, has blessed us.
[7] May God bless us, and let him be feared
   to the very ends of the earth.

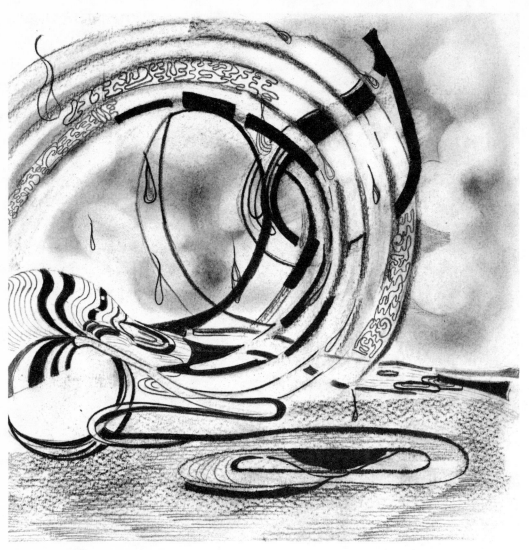

God, you rained a downpour of blessings, / when your heritage was faint you gave it strength;
(Psalm 68:9)

Psalm 68

For the choirmaster   Of David   Psalm   Song

NATIONAL SONG OF TRIUMPH

1 Let God arise, let his enemies be scattered,
  let those who hate him flee before him!
2 As smoke disperses, they disperse;
  as wax melts when near the fire,
  so the wicked perish when God approaches.

3 But at God's approach, the virtuous rejoice,
  exulting and singing for joy.
4 Sing to Yahweh, play music to his name,
  build a road for the Rider of the Clouds,
  rejoice in Yahweh, exult at his coming!

5 Father of orphans, defender of widows,
  such is God in his holy dwelling;
6 God gives the lonely a permanent home,
  makes prisoners happy by setting them free,
  but rebels must live in an arid land.

7 God, when you set out at the head of your people,
8 and marched across the desert, ·the earth rocked,   *Pause*

  the heavens deluged at God's coming,
  at the coming of God, the God of Israel.
9 God, you rained a downpour of blessings,
  when your heritage was faint you gave it strength;
10 your family found a home, where you
  in your goodness, God, provided for the needy.

11a The Lord gives his couriers the news,
14a "Shaddai has scattered ·a huge army."
12 Kings are in flight, armies in flight,
  the women at home take their pick of the loot.

13 Meanwhile you others were lolling in the sheepfolds.
  There were dove wings covered with silver,
  on their pinions the sheen of green gold;
14b jewels were there like snow on Dark Mountain.

15 That peak of Bashan, a mountain of God?
  Rather, a mountain of pride, that peak of Bashan!
16 Peaks of pride, have you the right to look down on

a mountain where God has chosen to live,
where Yahweh is going to live for ever?

[17] With thousands of myriads of divine chariots
the Lord has left Sinai for his sanctuary.
[18] God, you have ascended to the height, and captured prisoners,
you have taken men as tribute,
yes, taken rebels to your dwelling, Yahweh!

[19] Blessed be the Lord day after day,
the God who saves us and bears our burdens!
[20] This God of ours is a God who saves,
to the Lord Yahweh belong the ways of escape from death;
[21] but God will smash the heads of his enemies,
the hairy skull of the man who parades his guilt.

[22] The Lord has promised, "I will bring them back from Bashan,
I will bring them back from the bottom of the sea,
[23] for your feet to wade in blood,
for the tongues of your dogs to lap their share of the enemy."

[24] God, your procession can be seen,
my God's, my king's procession to the sanctuary,
[25] with cantors marching in front, musicians behind,
and between them maidens playing tambourines.

[26] Bless God in your choirs,
bless the Lord, you who spring from Israel!

[27] Benjamin, the youngest, is there in the lead,
the princes of Judah in brocaded robes,
the princes of Zebulun, the princes of Naphtali.

[28] Take command, God, as befits your power,
that power, God, you have wielded on our behalf
[29] from your Temple high above Jerusalem!
Kings will come to you, bringing presents.

[30] Rebuke the Beast of the Reeds,
that herd of bulls, those calves, that people,
until, humbled, they bring gold and silver.
Scatter those warmongering pagans!

[31] Ambassadors will come from Egypt,
Ethiopia will stretch out her hands to God.

[32] Sing to God, you kingdoms of the earth,
[33] play for ·the Rider of the Heavens, the ancient heavens!   *Pause*
Listen to him shouting, to his thundering,
[34] and acknowledge the power of God!

Over Israel his splendor, in the clouds his power,
35 God in his sanctuary is greatly to be feared.
He, the God of Israel,
gives power and strength to his people.
Blessed be God.

I am sinking in the deepest swamp, / there is no foothold; / I have stepped into deep water / and the waves are washing over me. (Psalm 69:2)

Psalm 69

For the choirmaster   Tune: "Lilies . . ."   Of David

LAMENT

¹ Save me, God! The water
   is already up to my neck!
² I am sinking in the deepest swamp,
   there is no foothold;
 I have stepped into deep water
   and the waves are washing over me.

³ Worn out with calling, my throat is hoarse,
 my eyes are strained, looking for my God.

⁴ More people hate me for no reason
   than I have hairs on my head,
 more are groundlessly hostile
   than I have hair to show.
 (They ask me to give back what I never took.)

⁵ God, you know how foolish I have been,
 my offenses are not hidden from you;

⁶ but let those who hope in you not blush for me,
   Yahweh Sabaoth!
 Let those who seek you not be ashamed of me,
   God of Israel!

⁷ It is for you I am putting up with insults
 that cover me with shame,
⁸ that make me a stranger to my brothers,
 an alien to my mother's other sons;
⁹ zeal for your house devours me,
 and the insults of those who insult you fall on me.

¹⁰ If I mortify myself with fasting,
 they make this a pretext for insulting me;
¹¹ if I dress myself in sackcloth,
 I become their laughingstock,
¹² the gossip of people sitting at the city gate,
 and the theme of drunken songs.

¹³ For my part, I pray to you, Yahweh,
   at the time you wish;
 in your great love, answer me, God,
   faithful in saving power.

¹⁴ Pull me out of this swamp; let me sink no further,
　　let me escape those who hate me,
　　　save me from deep water!
¹⁵ Do not let the waves wash over me,
　　do not let the deep swallow me
　or the Pit close its mouth on me.

¹⁶ In your loving kindness, answer me, Yahweh,
　　in your great tenderness turn to me;
¹⁷ do not hide your face from your servant,
　　quick, I am in trouble, answer me;
¹⁸ come to my side, redeem me,
　　from so many enemies ransom me.

^{19a} You know all the insults I endure,
^{19c} every one of my oppressors is known to you;
^{20a} the insults have broken my heart,
^{19b} my shame and disgrace are past cure;
　　I had hoped for sympathy, but in vain,
^{20c} I found no one to console me.

²¹ They gave me poison to eat instead,
　　when I was thirsty they gave me vinegar to drink.

²² May their own table prove a trap for them,
　　and their plentiful supplies, a snare!
²³ may their eyes grow dim, go blind,
　　strike their loins with chronic palsy!

²⁴ Vent your fury on them,
　　let your burning anger overtake them;
²⁵ may their camp be reduced to ruin,
　　and their tents left unoccupied:
²⁶ for hounding a man after you had struck him,
　　for adding more wounds to those which you inflicted.

²⁷ Charge them with crime after crime,
　　deny them further access to your righteousness,
²⁸ blot them out of the book of life,
　　strike them off the roll of the virtuous!

²⁹ For myself, wounded wretch that I am,
　　by your saving power, God, lift me up!
³⁰ I will praise the name of God with a song,
　　I will extol him with my thanksgiving,
³¹ more pleasing to Yahweh than any ox
　　or bull with horn and hoof.

[32] Then, seeing this, the humble can rejoice:
   long life to your hearts, all you who seek for God!
[33] Yahweh will always hear those who are in need,
   will never scorn his captive people.
[34] Let heaven and earth acclaim him,
   the oceans and all that moves in them!

[35] For God will save Zion,
   and rebuild the towns of Judah:
   they will be lived in, owned,
[36] handed down to his servants' descendants,
   and lived in by those who love his name.

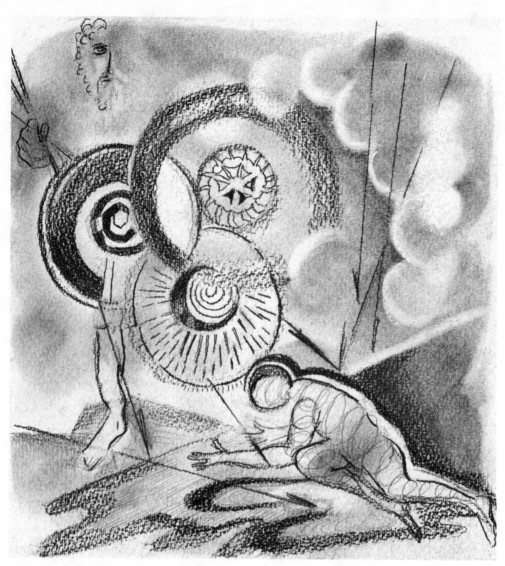

To me, poor wretch, / come quickly, God! / My helper, my savior, Yah-weh, / come without delay!
(*Psalm* 70:5)

Psalm 70

For the choirmaster   Of David   For commemoration

A CRY OF DISTRESS

[1] Oh come and rescue me, God,
    Yahweh come quickly and help me!
[2] Shame and dishonor on those
    who are out to kill me!

Down with them! Disgrace on those
    who enjoy my misfortune!
[3] May they be aghast with shame,
    those who say to me, "Aha! Aha!"

[4] But joy and gladness
    for all who seek you!
To all who love your saving power
    give constant cause to say, "God is great!"

[5] To me, poor wretch,
    come quickly, God!
My helper, my savior, Yahweh,
    come without delay!

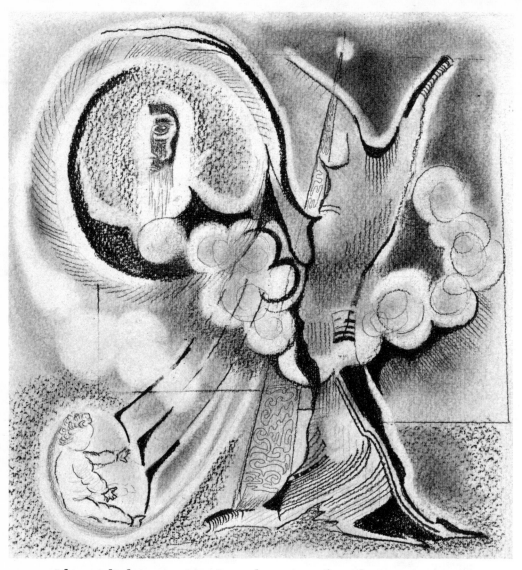

I have relied on you since I was born, / you have been my portion from my mother's womb, / and the constant theme of my praise. (Psalm 71:6)

Psalm 71

AN OLD MAN'S PRAYER

¹ In you, Yahweh, I take shelter;
  never let me be disgraced.
² In your righteousness rescue me, deliver me,
  turn your ear to me and save me!

³ Be a sheltering rock for me,
  a walled fortress to save me!
  For you are my rock, my fortress.
⁴ My God, rescue me from the hands of the wicked,
  from the clutches of rogue and tyrant!

⁵ For you alone are my hope, Lord,
  Yahweh, I have trusted you since my youth,
⁶ I have relied on you since I was born,
  you have been my portion from my mother's womb,
  and the constant theme of my praise.

⁷ To many I have seemed an enigma,
  but you are my firm refuge.
⁸ My mouth is full of your praises,
  filled with your splendor all day long.

⁹ Do not reject me now I am old,
  nor desert me now my strength is failing,
¹⁰ for my enemies are uttering threats,
  spies hatching their conspiracy:

¹¹ "Hound him down now that God has deserted him,
  seize him, there is no one to rescue him!"
¹² God, do not stand aside,
  my God, come quickly and help me!

¹³ Shame and ruin on those
    who attack me;
  may insult and disgrace cover those
    whose aim is to hurt me!

¹⁴ I promise that, ever hopeful,
    I will praise you more and more,
¹⁵ my lips shall proclaim your righteousness
    and power to save, all day long.

¹⁶ I will come in the power of Yahweh
  to commemorate your righteousness, yours alone.

¹⁷ God, you taught me when I was young,
  and I am still proclaiming your marvels.

¹⁸ Now that I am old and gray,
  God, do not desert me;
  let me live to tell the rising generation
  about your strength and power,
¹⁹ about your heavenly righteousness, God.

  You have done great things;
  who, God, is comparable to you?
²⁰ You have sent me misery and hardship,
  but you will give me life again,
  you will pull me up again from the depths of the earth,
²¹ prolong my old age, and once more comfort me.

²² I promise I will thank you on the lyre,
    my ever-faithful God,
  I will play the harp in your honor,
    Holy One of Israel.

²³ My lips shall sing for joy as I play to you,
    and this soul of mine which you have redeemed.
²⁴ And all day long, my tongue
    shall be talking of your righteousness.
  Shame and disgrace on those
    whose aim is to hurt me!

Let the mountains and hills / bring a message of peace for the people.
(Psalm 72:3)

Psalm 72

Of Solomon

THE PROMISED KING

¹ God, give your own justice to the king,
  your own righteousness to the royal son,
² so that he may rule your people rightly
  and your poor with justice.

³ Let the mountains and hills
  bring a message of peace for the people.
⁴ Uprightly ·he will defend the poorest,
 he will save the children of those in need,
  and crush their oppressors.

⁵ Like sun and moon he will endure,
  age after age,
⁶ welcome as rain that falls on the pasture,
  and showers to thirsty soil.

⁷ In his days virtue will flourish,
  a universal peace till the moon is no more;
⁸ his empire shall stretch from sea to sea,
  from the river to the ends of the earth.

⁹ The Beast will cower before him
  and his enemies grovel in the dust;
¹⁰ the kings of Tarshish and of the islands
  will pay him tribute.

 The kings of Sheba and Seba
  will offer gifts;
¹¹ all kings will do him homage,
  all nations become his servants.

¹² He will free the poor man who calls to him,
  and those who need help,
¹³ he will have pity on the poor and feeble,
  and save the lives of those in need;

¹⁴ he will redeem their lives from exploitation and outrage,
  their lives will be precious in his sight.
¹⁵ (Long may he live, may gold from Sheba be given him!)
 Prayer will be offered for him constantly,
  blessings invoked on him all day long.

[16] Grain everywhere in the country,
    even on the mountain tops,
abundant as Lebanon its harvest,
    luxuriant as common grass!

[17] Blessed be his name for ever,
    enduring as long as the sun!
May every race in the world be blessed in him,
    and all the nations call him blessed!

[18] Blessed be Yahweh, the God of Israel,
    who alone performs these marvels!
[19] Blessed for ever be his glorious name,
    may the whole world be filled with his glory!
        Amen. Amen!

[20] End of the prayers of David, son of Jesse.

Even so, I stayed in your presence, / you held my right hand;
(Psalm 73:23)

Psalm 73

Psalm   Of Asaph

THE TRIUMPH OF JUSTICE

[1] God is indeed good to Israel,
the Lord is good to pure hearts.

[2] My feet were on the point of stumbling,
a little further and I should have slipped,
[3] envying the arrogant as I did,
and watching the wicked get rich.

[4] For them, no such thing as pain,
their bodies are healthy and strong,
[5] they do not suffer as other men do,
no human afflictions for them!

[6] So pride is their chain of honor,
violence the garment that covers them;
[7] their spite oozes like fat,
their hearts drip with slyness.

[8] Cynical advocates of evil,
lofty advocates of force,
[9] they think their mouth is heaven
and their tongue can dictate on earth.

[10] This is why my people turn to them
and lap up all they say,
[11] asking, "How will God find out?
Does the Most High know everything?
[12] Look at them: these are the wicked,
well-off and still getting richer!"

[13] After all, why should I keep my own heart pure,
and wash my hands in innocence,
[14] if you plague me all day long
and discipline me every morning?

[15] Had I said, "That talk appeals to me,"
I should have betrayed your children's race.
[16] Instead, I tried to analyze the problem,
hard though I found it—

[17] until the day I pierced the mystery
and saw the end in store for them:

¹⁸ they are on a slippery slope, you put them there,
   you urge them on to ruin,

¹⁹ until suddenly they fall,
   done for, terrified to death.
²⁰ When you wake up, Lord, you shrug them off
   like the phantoms of a morning dream.

²¹ When my heart had been growing sourer
   with pains shooting through my loins,
²² I had simply failed to understand,
   my stupid attitude to you was brutish.

²³ Even so, I stayed in your presence,
   you held my right hand;
²⁴ now guide me with advice
   and in the end receive me into glory.

²⁵ I look to no one else in heaven,
   I delight in nothing else on earth.
²⁶ My flesh and my heart are pining with love,
   my heart's Rock, my own, God for ever!

²⁷ So then: those who abandon you are doomed,
   you destroy the adulterous deserter,
²⁸ whereas my joy lies in being close to God.
   I have taken shelter in the Lord,
   continually to proclaim what you have done.

Psalm 74

Poem   Of Asaph

LAMENT ON THE DESTRUCTION OF THE TEMPLE

[1] God, have you finally rejected us,
raging at the flock you used to pasture?
[2] Remember the people you long since made your own,
your hereditary tribe whom you redeemed,
and this Mount Zion where you came to live.

[3] Pick your steps over these endless ruins:
the enemy have sacked everything in the sanctuary.
[4] They roared where your Assemblies used to take place,
they stuck their enemy emblems over the entrance,
[5] emblems ·we had never seen before.

[6] Axes deep in the wood, ·hacking at the panels,
they battered them down with mallet and hatchet;
[7] then, God, setting fire to your sanctuary,
they profanely razed the house of your name to the ground.

[8] Determined to destroy us once and for all,
they burned down every shrine of God in the country.
[9] Deprived of signs, with no prophets left,
who can say how long this will last?

[10] How much longer, God, is the oppressor to blaspheme,
is the enemy to insult your name for ever?
[11] Why hold back your hand,
why keep your right hand hidden?

[12] Yet, God, my king from the first,
author of saving acts throughout the earth,
[13] by your power you split the sea in two,
and smashed the heads of monsters on the waters.

[14] You crushed Leviathan's heads,
leaving him for wild animals to eat,
[15] you opened the spring, the torrent,
you dried up inexhaustible rivers.

[16] You are master of day and night,
you instituted light and sun,
[17] you fixed the boundaries of the world,
you created summer and winter.

[18] Now, Yahweh, remember the enemy's blasphemy,
how frenzied people dare to insult your name.

by your power you split the sea in two, / and smashed the heads of monsters on the waters.
(*Psalm 74:13*)

19 Do not betray your turtledove to the beast,
    do not forget your wretched people for good.

20 Respect the covenant! We can bear no more—
    every cave in the country is the scene of violence!
21 Do not let the hard-pressed retreat in confusion,
    give the poor and needy cause to praise your name.

22 Rise, God, say something on your own behalf,
    do not forget the madman's daylong blaspheming,
23 remember the shouting of your enemies,
    this ever-rising clamor of your adversaries.

the earth shall quake and all its inhabitants, / it is I who poised its columns.
(*Psalm* 75:3)

Psalm 75

For the choirmaster   Tune: "Do not destroy"   Psalm   Of Asaph   Song

TO THE DIVINE JUDGE

[1] We give thanks to you, God,
  we give thanks as we invoke your name,
  as we recount your marvels.

[2] "At the moment I decide
  I will dispense strict justice;
[3] the earth shall quake and all its inhabitants,
  it is I who poised its columns.

[4] "I said to the boastful: Enough of boasting!
  and to the wicked: How dare you raise your horn,
[5] how dare you raise your horn like that,
  how dare you speak so boldly!"

[6] Not from the east, nor from the west,
  not from the desert, nor from the mountains,
[7] but from God the judgment comes,
  lowering one, raising another.

[8] Yahweh is holding a cup
  of frothing wine, heavily drugged;
  he pours it out, they drain it to the dregs,
  all drink of it, the wicked of the earth.

[9] But I will never stop proclaiming the God of Jacob
  or playing in his honor;
[10] I will cut off the horns of all the wicked
  and raise the horns of the virtuous.

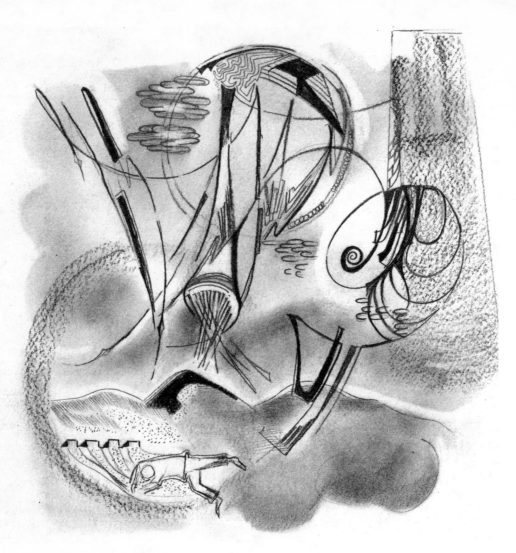

When your verdicts thunder from heaven, / earth stays silent with dread;
(Psalm 76:8)

Psalm 76

For the choirmaster For strings Psalm Of Asaph

ODE TO GOD THE AWE-INSPIRING

¹ God is renowned in Judah,
  his name is great in Israel;
² his tent is pitched in Salem,
  his home is in Zion;
³ there he has broken the lightning-swift arrow,
  the shield, the sword and the line of battle. *Pause*

⁴ You the Illustrious and Majestic:
⁵ mountains of spoil ·have been captured;
  heroes are now sleeping their last sleep,
  the warriors' arms have failed them;
⁶ at your reproof, God of Jacob,
  chariot and horse stand spellbound.

⁷ You the Terrible! Who can oppose you
  and your furious onslaught?
⁸ When your verdicts thunder from heaven,
  earth stays silent with dread;
⁹ when God stands up to give judgment
  and to save all the humble of the earth. *Pause*

¹⁰ Man's wrath only adds to your glory;
  the survivors of your wrath you will draw like a girdle around you;
¹¹ fulfill the promises you make to Yahweh your God,
  make offerings to the Terrible, you who surround him;
¹² he snuffs out the lives of princes,
  he is terrible to the kings of the earth.

Psalm 77

For the choirmaster . . . Jeduthun Of Asaph Psalm

MEDITATION ON ISRAEL'S PAST

¹ Loudly I cry to God,
  loudly to God who hears me.

² When in trouble I sought the Lord,
  all night long I stretched out my hands,
  my soul refusing to be consoled.
³ I thought of God and sighed,
  I pondered and my spirit failed me.

⁴ You stopped me closing my eyes,
  I was too distraught to speak;
⁵ I thought of the olden days,
⁶ years long past ·came back to me,
  I spent all night meditating in my heart,
  I pondered and my spirit asked this question:

⁷ "If the Lord has rejected you, is this final?
  If he withholds his favor, is this for ever?
⁸ Is his love over for good
  and the promise void for all time?
⁹ Has God forgotten to show mercy,
  or has his anger overcome his tenderness? *Pause*

¹⁰ "This," I said then, "is what distresses me:
  that the power of the Most High is no longer what it was."
¹¹ Remembering Yahweh's achievements,
  remembering your marvels in the past,
¹² I reflect on all that you did,
  I ponder on all your achievements.

¹³ God, your ways are holy!
  What god so great as God?
¹⁴ You are the God who did marvelous things
  and forced nations to acknowledge your power,
¹⁵ with your own arm redeeming your people,
  the sons of Jacob and Joseph. *Pause*

¹⁶ When the waters saw it was you, God,
  when the waters saw it was you, they recoiled,
  shuddering to their depths.
¹⁷ The clouds poured down water,
  the sky thundered,
  your arrows darted out.

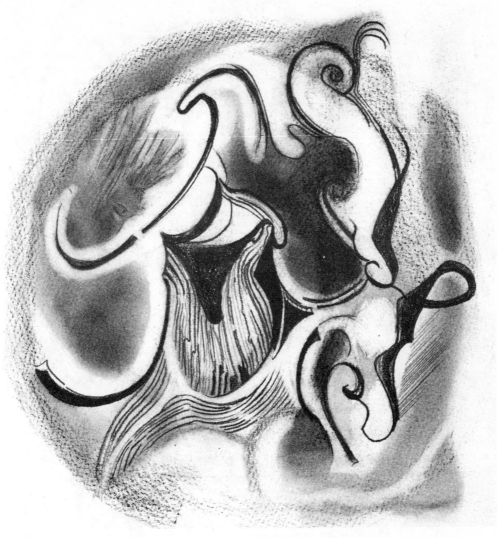

When the waters saw it was you, God, / when the waters saw it was you, they recoiled, / shuddering to their depths.
(*Psalm 77:16*)

[18] Your thunder crashed as it rolled,
  your lightning lit up the world,
  the earth shuddered and quaked.
[19] You strode across the sea,
  you marched across the ocean,
  but your steps could not be seen.

[20] You guided your people like a flock
  by the hands of Moses and Aaron.

I am going to speak to you in parable / and expound the mysteries of our past.
(*Psalm 78:2*)

Psalm 78

Psalm   Of Asaph

THE LESSONS OF ISRAELITE HISTORY

[1] Listen to this Law, my people,
  pay attention to what I say;
[2] I am going to speak to you in parable
  and expound the mysteries of our past.

[3] What we have heard and known for ourselves,
  and what our ancestors have told us,
[4] must not be withheld from their descendants,
  but be handed on by us to the next generation;

  that is: the titles of Yahweh, his power
  and the miracles he has done.
[5] When he issued the decrees for Jacob
  and instituted a Law in Israel,

  he gave our ancestors strict orders
  to teach it to their children;
[6] the next generation was to learn it,
  the children still to be born,

  and these in their turn were to tell their own children
[7] so that they too would put their confidence in God,
  never forgetting God's achievements,
  and always keeping his commandments,

[8] and not becoming, like their ancestors,
  a stubborn and unruly generation,
  a generation with no sincerity of heart,
  in spirit unfaithful to God.

[9] The sons of Ephraim, who were bowmen,
  turned tail when the time came to fight;
[10] they have not kept God's covenant,
  they refused to follow his Law;

[11] they had forgotten his achievements,
  the marvels he had shown them:
[12] he had worked wonders for their ancestors
  in the plains of Zoan, down in Egypt:

[13] dividing the sea, bringing them through,
  making the waters stand up like dikes,

¹⁴ leading them with a cloud by day
and with a fiery glow at night,

¹⁵ splitting rocks in the wilderness,
quenching their thirst with unlimited water,
¹⁶ conjuring streams from the rock
and bringing down water in torrents.

¹⁷ They only sinned against him more than ever,
defying the Most High in the desert,
¹⁸ deliberately challenging God
by demanding their favorite food.

¹⁹ They blasphemed against God,
"Is it likely," they said, "that God
could give a banquet in the wilderness?

²⁰ "Admittedly, when he struck the rock,
waters gushed, torrents streamed out,
but bread now, can he give us that,
can he provide meat for his people?"

²¹ Yahweh was enraged when he heard them,
a fire flared at Jacob,
the wrath attacked Israel
²² for having no faith in God,
no trust in his power to save.

²³ He gave orders to the skies above,
he opened the doors of heaven,
²⁴ he rained down manna to feed them,
he gave them the wheat of heaven;
²⁵ men ate the bread of Immortals,
he sent them more food than they could eat.

²⁶ He stirred up an east wind in the heavens,
he conjured up a south wind by his power,
²⁷ he rained down meat on them like dust;
birds as thick as sand on the seashore
²⁸ he sent tumbling into their camp,
in all directions around their tents.

²⁹ They all had enough and to spare,
he having provided what they wanted;
³⁰ but they had hardly satisfied their craving,
the food was still in their mouths,

³¹ when the wrath of God attacked them,
slaughtering their strongest men
and laying the flower of Israel low.

32 Despite all this they went on sinning,
   and put no faith in his marvels;
33 for which he blasted their days
   and their years in a flash.

34 Whenever he slaughtered them they sought him,
   they came to their senses and sought him earnestly
35 remembering that God was their rock,
   God the Most High, their redeemer.

36 But though they outwardly flattered him
   and used their tongues to lie to him,
37 in their hearts they were not true to him,
   they were unfaithful to his covenant.

38 Compassionately, however,
   he forgave their guilt instead of killing them,
   repeatedly repressing his anger
   instead of rousing his full wrath,
39 remembering they were creatures of flesh,
   a puff of wind that passes and does not return.

40 How often they defied him in the wilderness,
   how often they outraged him in the desert,
41 repeatedly challenging God,
   provoking the Holy One of Israel—
42 entirely oblivious of his hand
   and of the time he saved them from the oppressor:

43 by imposing his signs on Egypt,
   by displaying his wonders in the plains of Zoan,
44 by turning their rivers into blood
   to stop them drinking from their streams,

45 by sending horseflies to eat them
   and frogs to devastate them,
46 by consigning their crops to the caterpillar
   and their hard-won harvest to the locust,

47 by killing their vines with hail
   and their sycamore trees with frost,
48 by condemning their cattle to plague
   and their flocks to feverish pests,

49 by unleashing his fierce anger, rage,
   indignation and hardship on them,
   a mission of angels of disaster,
50 by giving his anger free rein,

by not even exempting them from death,
　by condemning them to plague,
⁵¹ by striking down all the first-born in Egypt,
　the first fruits of their virility in the tents of Ham,

⁵² by driving his people out like sheep,
　by leading them through the wilderness like a flock,
⁵³ by guiding them safe and unafraid
　while the sea engulfed their enemies,

⁵⁴ by bringing them to his sacred frontier,
　the highlands conquered by his own right hand,
⁵⁵ by expelling the pagans in front of them
　and by marking out a heritage for each,
　in which the tribes of Israel could pitch their tents.

⁵⁶ Even so, they went on challenging God the Most High,
　rebelliously disregarding his decrees;
⁵⁷ as perverse and disloyal as their ancestors,
　treacherous as a bow with a warp,
⁵⁸ provoking him with their high places
　and rousing his jealousy with their idols.

⁵⁹ God was enraged when he heard them,
　he rejected Israel out of hand,
⁶⁰ he left his home in Shiloh,
　that tent where he once lived with men.

⁶¹ He consigned his power to captivity,
　his splendor to the enemy's clutches;
⁶² he condemned his own people to the sword,
　he raged at his heritage,

⁶³ whose young men were then burned to death—
　no brides left to hear the wedding song;
⁶⁴ whose priests fell by the sword—
　no widows left to raise the dirge.

⁶⁵ Then, like a sleeper, like a hero
　fighting-mad with wine, the Lord woke up
⁶⁶ to strike his enemies on the rump
　and put them to everlasting shame.

⁶⁷ Rejecting the tent of Joseph,
　not choosing the tribe of Ephraim,
⁶⁸ instead he chose the tribe of Judah
　and his well-loved mountain of Zion,
⁶⁹ where he built his sanctuary, a copy of high heaven,
　founding it firm as the earth for ever.

[70] Choosing David as his servant,
   he took him from the sheepfolds,
[71] called him from tending ewes in lamb
   and pasture his people Jacob
   and Israel his heritage:
[72] who did this with unselfish care
   and led them with a sensitive hand.

God, the pagans have invaded your heritage, / they have desecrated your holy Temple; / they have reduced Jerusalem to a pile of ruins, (Psalm 79:1)

Psalm 79

Psalm   Of   Asaph

NATIONAL LAMENT

[1] God, the pagans have invaded your heritage,
  they have desecrated your holy Temple;
  they have reduced Jerusalem to a pile of ruins,
[2] they have left the corpses of your servants
  to the birds of the air for food,
  and the flesh of your devout to the beasts of the earth.

[3] They have shed blood like water
  throughout Jerusalem, not a gravedigger left!
[4] we are now insulted by our neighbors,
  butt and laughingstock of all those around us.
[5] How much longer will you be angry, Yahweh? For ever?
  Is your jealously to go on smoldering like a fire?

[6] Pour out your anger on the pagans,
    who do not acknowledge you,
  and on those kingdoms
    that do not call on your name,
[7] for they have devoured Jacob
    and reduced his home to desolation.

[8] Do not hold our ancestors' crimes against us,
  in tenderness quickly intervene,
  we can hardly be crushed lower;
[9] help us, God our savior,
  for the honor of your name;
  Yahweh, blot out our sins,
  rescue us for the sake of your name.

[10] Why should the pagans ask, "Where is their God?"
  May we soon see the pagans learning what vengeance
  you exact for your servants' blood shed here!
[11] May the groans of the captive reach you;
  by your mighty arm rescue those doomed to die!

[12] Pay our neighbors sevenfold, strike to the heart
  for the monstrous insult proffered to you, Lord!
[13] And we your people, the flock that you pasture,
    giving you everlasting thanks,
    will recite your praises for ever and ever.

Psalm 80

For the choirmaster   Tune: "The decrees are lilies"   Of Asaph   Psalm

PRAYER FOR THE RESTORATION OF ISRAEL

¹ Shepherd of Israel, listen,
    you who lead Joseph like a flock;
    enthroned on the cherubs, shine
² on Ephraim, Benjamin and Manasseh;
    rouse your strength,
    come to us and save us!

³ Yahweh Sabaoth, bring us back,
    let your face smile on us and we shall be safe.

⁴ Yahweh Sabaoth, how much longer
    will you smolder at your people's prayer?
⁵ Having fed us on the bread of tears,
    having made us drink them in such measure,
⁶ you now let our neighbors quarrel over us
    and our enemies deride us.

⁷ Yahweh Sabaoth, bring us back,
    let your face smile on us and we shall be safe.

⁸ There was a vine: you uprooted it from Egypt;
    to plant it, you drove out other nations,
⁹ you cleared a space where it could grow,
    it took root and filled the whole country.

¹⁰ It covered the mountains with its shade,
    the cedars of God with its branches,
¹¹ its tendrils extended to the sea,
    its offshoots all the way to the river.

¹² Why have you destroyed its fences?
    Now anyone can go and steal its grapes,
¹³ the forest boar can ravage it
    and wild animals eat it.

¹⁴ Please, Yahweh Sabaoth, relent!
    Look down from heaven, look at this vine,
¹⁵ visit it, ·protect
    what your own right hand has planted.
¹⁶ They threw it on the fire like dung,
    but one look of reproof from you
    and they will be doomed.

It covered the mountains with its shade, / the cedars of God with its branches,
(*Psalm 80:10*)

[17] May your hand protect the man at your right,
the son of man who has been authorized by you.
[18] We shall never turn from you again;
our life renewed, we shall invoke your name.

[19] Yahweh Sabaoth, bring us back,
let your face smile on us and we shall be safe.

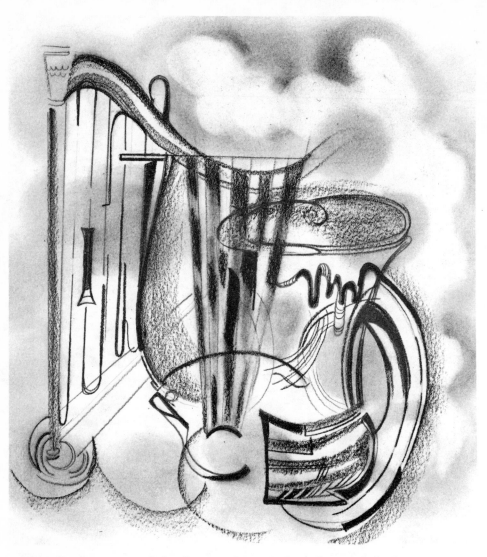

Start the music, sound the drum, / the melodious lyre and the harp;
(*Psalm 81:2*)

Psalm 81

For the choirmaster On the . . . of Gath Of Asaph

FOR THE FEAST OF TABERNACLES

[1] Shout for joy to honor God our strength,
shout to acclaim the God of Jacob!

[2] Start the music, sound the drum,
the melodious lyre and the harp;
[3] sound the New Moon trumpet,
at the full moon, on our feast day!

[4] This is a statute binding on Israel,
an ordinance of the God of Jacob,
[5] this decree he imposed on Joseph
when he went to war against Egypt.

I can hear a voice I no longer recognize,
[6] "It was I who relieved your shoulder of the burden,
your hands could drop the laborer's basket;
[7] you called in your trouble, so I rescued you.

"Hidden in the storm, I answered you,
I tested you at the waters of Meribah.   *Pause*
[8] Listen, you are my people, let me warn you.
Israel, if you would only listen to me!

[9] "Tolerate no foreign god,
worship no alien god;
[10] I, Yahweh, am your God,
I who brought you here from Egypt;
you have only to open your mouth for me to fill it.

[11] "My people refused to listen to me,
Israel refused to obey me,
[12] so I left them to their stubborn selves
to do whatever they pleased.

[13] "If only my people would listen,
if Israel would follow my ways,
[14] at one blow I would defeat their enemies
and strike at all who attack them.

[15] "Then those who hate Yahweh would cringe,
their doom being sealed for ever;
[16] while I would feed you on pure wheat
and satisfy you with the wild rock honey."

Rise, God, dispense justice throughout the world, / since no nation is excluded from your ownership.
(Psalm 82:8)

Psalm 82

Psalm   of Asaph

AGAINST CORRUPT JUDGES

[1] God stands in the divine assembly,
among the gods he dispenses justice:

[2] "No more mockery of justice,
no more favoring the wicked!   *Pause*
[3] Let the weak and the orphan have justice,
be fair to the wretched and destitute;
[4] rescue the weak and needy,
save them from the clutches of the wicked!"

[5] Ignorant and senseless, they carry on blindly,
undermining the very basis of earthly society.
[6] I once said, "You too are gods,
sons of the Most High, all of you,"
[7] but all the same, you shall die like other men;
as one man, princes, you shall fall.

[8] Rise, God, dispense justice throughout the world,
since no nation is excluded from your ownership.

Psalm 83

Song   Psalm   Of Asaph

AGAINST THE ENEMIES OF ISRAEL

¹ God, do not remain silent;
   do not be unmoved, O God, or unresponsive!
² See how your enemies are stirring,
   see how those who hate you rear their heads.

³ Weaving a plot against your people,
⁴ conspiring against those you protect, ·they say,
   "Come, we will finish them as a nation,
   the name of Israel shall be forgotten!"

⁵ Unanimous in their plot,
   they seal a treaty against you:
⁶ the tents of Edom and the Ishmaelites,
   Moab and the Hagrites,

⁷ Gebal, Ammon, Amalek,
   Philistia and the Tyrians;
⁸ and now Assur has joined them
   to reinforce the sons of Lot.   *Pause*

⁹ Treat them like Midian and Sisera,
   like Jabin at the river Kishon,
¹⁰ wiped out at En-dor,
   they served to dung the ground.

¹¹ Treat their generals like Oreb and Zeeb,
   their commanders like Zebah and Zalmunna,
¹² those who once said, "Let us take for ourselves
   possession of the Dwellings of God!"

¹³ My God, bowl them along like tumbleweed,
   like chaff at the mercy of the wind;
¹⁴ as fire devours the forest,
   as the flame licks up the mountains,

¹⁵ drive them on with your whirlwind,
   rout them with your tornado;
¹⁶ cover their faces with shame,
   until they seek your name, Yahweh.

drive them on with your whirlwind, / rout them with your tornado;
(Psalm 83:15)

[17] Shame and panic be always theirs,
[18] disgrace and death; ·and let them know this:
  you alone bear the name Yahweh,
  Most High over the whole world.

A single day in your courts / is worth more than a thousand else-
where; / merely to stand on the steps of God's house / is better than
living with the wicked.
(Psalm 84:10)

Psalm 84

For the choirmaster On the . . . of Gath Of the sons of Korah
Psalm

PILGRIMAGE SONG

¹ How I love your palace,
  Yahweh Sabaoth!
² How my soul yearns and pines
  for Yahweh's courts!
My heart and my flesh sing for joy
  to the living God.

³ The sparrow has found its home at last,
the swallow a nest for its young,
your altars, Yahweh Sabaoth,
  my king and my God.

⁴ Happy those who live in your house
  and can praise you all day long; *Pause*
⁵ and happy the pilgrims inspired by you
  with courage to make the Ascents!

⁶ As they go through the Valley of the Weeper,
  they make it a place of springs,
clothed in blessings by early rains.
⁷ Thence they make their way from height to height,
  soon to be seen before God on Zion.

⁸ Yahweh Sabaoth, hear my prayer,
listen, God of Jacob; *Pause*
⁹ God our shield, now look on us
and be kind to your anointed.

¹⁰ A single day in your courts
  is worth more than a thousand elsewhere;
merely to stand on the steps of God's house
  is better than living with the wicked.

¹¹ For God is battlement and shield,
  conferring grace and glory;
Yahweh withholds nothing good
  from those who walk without blame.

¹²   Yahweh Sabaoth,
happy the man who puts his trust in you!

Yahweh, you favor your own country, / you bring back the captives of Jacob,
(*Psalm 85:1*)

Psalm 85

For the choirmaster Of the sons of Korah Psalm

PRAYER FOR PEACE

¹ Yahweh, you favor your own country,
   you bring back the captives of Jacob,
² you take your people's guilt away,
   you blot out all their sins,   *Pause*
³ you retract all your anger,
   you abjure your fiery rage.

⁴ Bring us back, God our savior,
   master your resentment against us.
⁵ Do you mean to be angry with us for ever,
   to prolong your wrath age after age?

⁶ Will you not give us life again,
   for your people to rejoice in you?
⁷ Yahweh, show us your love,
   grant us your saving help.

⁸ I am listening. What is Yahweh saying?
   What God is saying means peace
   for his people, for his friends,
   if only they renounce their folly;
⁹ for those who fear him, his saving help is near,
   and the glory will then live in our country.

¹⁰ Love and Loyalty now meet,
   Righteousness and Peace now embrace;
¹¹ Loyalty reaches up from earth
   and Righteousness leans down from heaven.

¹² Yahweh himself bestows happiness
   as our soil gives its harvest,
¹³ Righteousness always preceding him
   and Peace following his footsteps.

Psalm 86

Prayer Of David

PRAYER IN ORDEAL

1 Listen to me, Yahweh, and answer me,
   poor and needy as I am;
2 keep my soul: I am your devoted one,
   save your servant who relies on you.

3 You are my God, ·take pity on me, Lord,
   I invoke you all day long;
4 give your servant reason to rejoice,
   for to you, Lord, I lift my soul.

5 Lord, you are good and forgiving,
   most loving to all who invoke you;
6 Yahweh, hear my prayer,
   listen to me as I plead.

7 Lord, in trouble I invoke you,
   and you answer my prayer;
8 there is no god to compare with you,
   no achievement to compare with yours.

9 All the pagans will come and adore you, Lord,
   all will glorify your name,
10 since you alone are great, you perform marvels,
   you God, you alone.

11 Yahweh, teach me your way,
   how to walk beside you faithfully,
   make me singlehearted in fearing your name.

12 I thank you with all my heart, Lord my God,
   I glorify your name for ever,
13 your love for me has been so great,
   you have rescued me from the depths of Sheol.

14 Now arrogant men, God, are attacking me,
   a brutal gang hounding me to death:
   people to whom you mean nothing.

15 Lord God, you who are always merciful and tenderhearted,
   slow to anger, always loving, always loyal,
16 turn to me and pity me.

Listen to me, Yahweh, and answer me, / poor and needy as I am;
(Psalm 86:1)

Give me your strength, your saving help,
me your servant, this son of a pious mother,
[17] give me one proof of your goodness.

Yahweh, make my opponents ashamed,
show them that you are my help and consolation.

Yahweh loves his city / founded on the holy mountain;
(*Psalm 87:1*)

Psalm 87

Of the sons of Korah   Psalm   Song

ZION, MOTHER OF NATIONS

²ᵃ Yahweh loves ·his city
    founded on the holy mountain;
²ᵇ he prefers the gates of Zion
²ᶜ   to any town in Jacob.
³ He has glorious predictions to make of you,
    city of God!   *Pause*

⁴ "I will add Egypt and Babylon
    to the nations that acknowledge me.
  Of Philistia, Tyre, Ethiopia,
    'Here so and so was born,' men say.
⁵ But all call Zion 'Mother,'
    since all were born in her."

  It is he who makes her what she is,
⁶   he, the Most High, ·Yahweh;
  and as he registers the peoples,
    "It was here," he writes, "that so and so was born."   *Pause*
⁷ And there will be princes dancing there.
    All find their home in you.

Psalm 88

*Song   Psalm   Of the sons of Korah   For the choirmaster   In sickness
or suffering   Poem   For Heman the native-born*

LAMENT

¹ Yahweh my God, I call for help all day,
  I weep to you all night;
² may my prayer reach you
  hear my cries for help;

³ for my soul is all troubled,
  my life is on the brink of Sheol;
⁴ I am numbered among those who go down to the Pit,
  a man bereft of strength:

⁵ a man alone, down among the dead,
  among the slaughtered in their graves,
  among those you have forgotten,
  those deprived of your protecting hand.

⁶ You have plunged me to the bottom of the Pit,
  to its darkest, deepest place,
⁷ weighted down by your anger,
  drowned beneath your waves.   *Pause*

⁸ You have turned my friends against me
  and made me repulsive to them;
  in prison and unable to escape,
⁹ my eyes are worn out with suffering.

  Yahweh, I invoke you all day,
  I stretch out my hands to you:
¹⁰ are your marvels meant for the dead,
  can ghosts rise up to praise you?   *Pause*

¹¹ Who talks of your love in the grave,
  of your faithfulness in the place of perdition?
¹² Do they hear about your marvels in the dark,
  about your righteousness in the land of oblivion?

¹³ But I am here, calling for your help,
  praying to you every morning:
¹⁴ why do you reject me?
  Why do you hide your face from me?

You have plunged me to the bottom of the Pit, / to its darkest, deepest place,
(*Psalm 88:6*)

[15] Wretched, slowly dying since my youth,
  I bore your terrors—now I am exhausted;
[16] your anger overwhelmed me,
  you destroyed me with your terrors
[17] which, like a flood, were around me, all day long,
  all together closing in on me.
[18] You have turned my friends and neighbors against me,
  now darkness is my one companion left.

Once you spoke in vision / and said to your friends, / "I have conferred the crown on a hero, / and promoted one chosen from my people. (Psalm 89:19)

Psalm 89

Poem   For Ethan the native-born

HYMN AND A PRAYER TO GOD'S FAITHFULNESS

¹ I will celebrate your love for ever, Yahweh,
  age after age my words shall proclaim your faithfulness;
² for I claim that love is built to last for ever
  and your faithfulness founded firmly in the heavens.

³   "I have made a covenant with my Chosen,
    I have given my servant David my sworn word:
⁴   I have founded your dynasty to last for ever,
    I have built you a throne to outlast all time."   *Pause*

⁵ Yahweh, the assembly of holy ones in heaven
  applaud the marvel of your faithfulness.
⁶ Who in the skies can compare with Yahweh?
  Which of the heaven-born can rival him?

⁷ God, dreaded in the assembly of holy ones,
  great and terrible to all around him,
⁸ Yahweh, God of Sabaoth, who is like you?—
  mighty Yahweh, clothed in your faithfulness!

⁹ You control the pride of the ocean,
  when its waves high, you calm them;
¹⁰ you split Rahab in two like a carcass
  and scattered your enemies with your mighty arm.

¹¹ The heavens are yours and the earth is yours,
  you founded the world and all it holds,
¹² you created north and south;
  Tabor and Hermon hail your name with joy.

¹³ Yours was the arm, and yours the prowess,
  mighty and exalted your right hand;
¹⁴ Righteousness and Justice support your throne,
  Love and Faithfulness are your attendants.

¹⁵ Happy the people who learn to acclaim you!
  Yahweh, they will live in the light of your favor;
¹⁶   they will rejoice in your name all day
    and exult in your righteousness.

¹⁷   You are their glory and their strength,
    you, by your kindness, raise our fortunes,

18   since both our shield and our king
      belong to Yahweh, the Holy One of Israel.

19   Once you spoke in vision
      and said to your friends,
      "I have conferred the crown on a hero,
      and promoted one chosen from my people.

20   "I have selected my servant David
      and anointed him with my holy oil;
21   my hand will be constantly with him,
      he will be able to rely on my arm.

22   "No enemy will be able to outwit him,
      no wicked man to worst him,
23   I myself will crush his opponents,
      I will strike dead all who hate him.

24   "With my faithfulness and love,
      his fortunes shall rise in my name.
25   I will give him control of the sea,
      complete control of the rivers.

26   "He will invoke me, 'My father,
      my God and rock of my safety,'
27   and I shall make him my first-born,
      the Most High for kings on earth.

28   "I will keep my love for him always,
      my covenant with him shall stand,
29   I have founded his dynasty to last for ever,
      his throne to be as lasting as the heavens.

30   "Should his descendants desert my Law
      and disregard my rulings,
31   should they violate my statutes
      and not keep my commandments,

32   "I will punish their sins with the rod
      and their crimes with the whip,
33   but never withdraw my love from him
      or fail in my faithfulness.

34   "I will not break my covenant,
      I will not revoke my given word;
35   I have sworn on my holiness, once for all,
      and cannot turn liar to David.

36   "His dynasty shall last for ever,
      I see his throne like the sun,

37   enduring for ever like the moon,
     that faithful witness in the sky." *Pause*

38   And yet you have rejected, disowned
     and raged at your anointed;
39   you have repudiated the covenant with your servant
     and flung his crown dishonored to the ground.

40   You have pierced all his defenses,
     and laid his forts in ruins;
41   anyone may go and loot him,
     his neighbors treat him with scorn.

42   You have let his opponents get the upper hand,
     and made all his enemies happy,
43   you have snapped his sword on a rock
     and failed to support him in battle.

44   You have stripped him of his glorious scepter,
     and toppled his throne to the ground,
45   you have aged him before his time
     and covered him in shame. *Pause*

46 Yahweh, how much longer will you hide? For ever?
  How much longer must your anger smolder like a fire?
47 Remember me, the short time I have left
  and the void to which you destine mankind.
48 What man can cling to life and not see death?
  Who can evade the clutches of Sheol? *Pause*

49 Lord, where are those earlier signs of your love?
  You swore your oath to David on your faithfulness!
50 Lord, do not forget how your servant was insulted,
  how I take these pagans' taunts to heart,
51 insults, Yahweh, that your enemies have offered,
  insults to your anointed wherever he goes.

    Blessed be Yahweh for ever.
      Amen. Amen!

Psalm 90

Prayer   Of Moses, man of God

THE HUMAN CONDITION

[1] Lord, you have been
   our refuge age after age.

[2] Before the mountains were born,
   before the earth or the world came to birth,
   you were God from all eternity and for ever.

[3] You can turn man back into dust
   by saying, "Back to what you were, you sons of men!"
[4] To you, a thousand years are a single day,
   a yesterday now over, an hour of the night.

[5] You brush men away like waking dreams,
   they are like grass
[6] sprouting and flowering in the morning,
   withered and dry before dusk.

[7] We too are burned up by your anger
   and terrified by your fury;
[8] having summoned up our sins
   you inspect our secrets by your own light.

[9] Our days dwindle under your wrath,
   our lives are over in a breath
[10] —our life lasts for seventy years,
   eighty with good health,

   but they all add up to anxiety and trouble—
   over in a trice, and then we are gone.
[11] Who yet has felt the full force of your fury,
   or learned to fear the violence of your rage?

[12] Teach us to count how few days we have
   and so gain wisdom of heart.
[13] Relent, Yahweh! How much longer do we have?
   Take pity on your servants!

[14] Let us wake in the morning filled with your love
   and sing and be happy all our days;
[15] make our future as happy as our past was sad,
   those years when you were punishing us.

—our life lasts for seventy years, / eighty with good health,
(Psalm 90:10)

[16] Let your servants see what you can do for them,
   let their children see your glory.
[17] May the sweetness of the Lord be on us!
   Make all we do succeed.

he covers you with his feathers, / and you find shelter underneath his wings.
(Psalm 91:4)

Psalm 91

GOD'S PROTECTION

1 If you live in the shelter of Elyon
  and make your home in the shadow of Shaddai,
2 you can say to Yahweh, "My refuge, my fortress,
  my God in whom I trust!"

3 He rescues you from the snares
  of fowlers hoping to destroy you;
4a he covers you with his feathers,
4b and you find shelter underneath his wings.

5 You need not fear the terrors of night,
  the arrow that flies in the daytime,
6 the plague that stalks in the dark,
  the scourge that wreaks havoc in broad daylight.

7 Though a thousand fall at your side,
  ten thousand at your right hand,
  you yourself will remain unscathed,
4c with his faithfulness for shield and buckler.

8 You have only to look around
  to see how the wicked are repaid,
9 you who can say, "Yahweh my refuge,"
  and make Elyon your fortress.

10 No disaster can overtake you,
  no plague come near your tent:
11 he will put you in his angels' charge
  to guard you wherever you go.

12 They will support you on their hands
  in case you hurt your foot against a stone;
13 you will tread on lion and adder,
  trample on savage lions and dragons.

14 "I rescue all who cling to me,
  I protect whoever knows my name,
15 I answer everyone who invokes me,
  I am with them when they are in trouble;
  I bring them safety and honor.
16 I give them life, long and full,
  and show them how I can save."

so the virtuous flourish like palm trees / and grow as tall as the cedars of Lebanon.
(*Psalm 92:12*)

Psalm 92

Psalm   Song   For the sabbath

THE VIRTUOUS MAN REJOICES

[1] It is good to give thanks to Yahweh,
to play in honor of your name, Most High,
[2] to proclaim your love at daybreak
and your faithfulness all through the night
[3] to the music of the zither and lyre,
to the rippling of the harp.

[4] I am happy, Yahweh, at what you have done;
at your achievements I joyfully exclaim,
[5] "Great are your achievements, Yahweh,
immensely deep your thoughts!"
[6] Stupid men are not aware of this,
fools can never appreciate it.

[7] The wicked may sprout as thick as weeds
and every evildoer flourish,
but only to be everlastingly destroyed,
[8] whereas you are supreme for ever.
[9] See how your enemies perish,
how all evil men are routed.

[10] You raise my horn as if I were a wild ox,
you pour fresh oil on my head;
[11] I was able to see those who were spying on me,
to overhear what the wicked were whispering,
[12] so the virtuous flourish like palm trees
and grow as tall as the cedars of Lebanon.

[13] Planted in the house of Yahweh,
they will flourish in the courts of our God,
[14] still bearing fruit in old age,
still remaining fresh and green,
[15] to proclaim that Yahweh is righteous,
my rock in whom no fault is to be found!

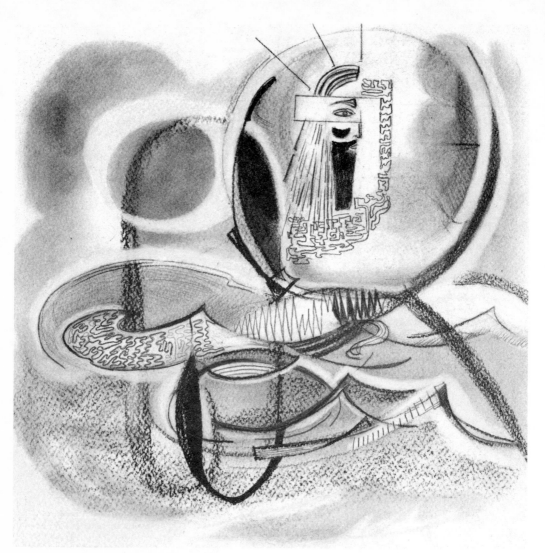

greater than the voice of ocean, / transcending the waves of the sea, / Yahweh reigns transcendent in the heights.
(*Psalm 93:4*)

Psalm 93

[1] Yahweh is king, robed in majesty,
Yahweh is robed in power,
he wears it like a belt.

You have made the world firm, unshakable;
[2] your throne has stood since then,
you existed from the first, Yahweh.

[3] Yahweh, the rivers raise,
the rivers raise their voices,
the rivers raise their thunders;

[4] greater than the voice of ocean,
transcending the waves of the sea,
Yahweh reigns transcendent in the heights.

[5] Your decrees will never alter;
holiness will distinguish your house,
Yahweh, for ever and ever.

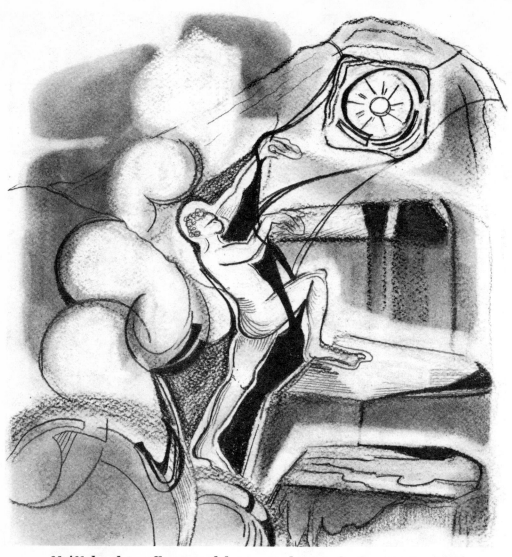

No! Yahweh is still my citadel, / my God is a rock where I take shelter;
(Psalm 94:22)

Psalm 94

1 Yahweh, God of revenge,
   God of revenge, appear!
2 Rise, judge of the world,
   give the proud their deserts!

3 Yahweh, how much longer are the wicked,
   how much longer are the wicked to triumph?
4 Are these evil men to remain unsilenced,
   boasting and asserting themselves?

5 Yahweh, they crush your people,
   they oppress your hereditary people,
6 murdering and massacring
   widows, orphans and guests.

7 "Yahweh sees nothing," they say,
   "the God of Jacob takes no notice."
8 You most stupid of men, you fools,
   think this over and learn some sense.

9 Is the inventor of the ear unable to hear?
   The creator of the eye unable to see?
10 The punisher of the pagans unable to punish?
   Yahweh the teacher of mankind
11 knows exactly how men think,
   how their thoughts are a puff of wind.

12 Yahweh, happy the man whom you instruct,
   the man whom you teach through your law;
13 his mind is at peace though times are bad,
   while a pit is being dug for the wicked.

14 For Yahweh has not abandoned
   or deserted his hereditary people;
15 for verdict will return to righteousness again,
   and, in its wake, all upright hearts.

16 No one ever stood up for me against the wicked,
   not a soul took a stand to save me from evil men;
17 without Yahweh's help, I should, long ago,
   have gone to the Home of Silence.

18 I need only say, "I am slipping,"
   and your love, Yahweh, immediately supports me;

19   and in the middle of all my troubles
     you console me and make me happy.

20   You never consent to that corrupt tribunal
     that imposes disorder as law,
21   that takes the life of the virtuous
     and condemns the innocent to death.

22   No! Yahweh is still my citadel,
     my God is a rock where I take shelter;
23   he will pay them back for all their sins,
     he will silence their wickedness,
   Yahweh our God will silence them.

Come in, let us bow, prostrate ourselves, / and kneel in front of Yahweh our maker,
(Psalm 95:6)

Psalm 95

[1] Come, let us praise Yahweh joyfully,
   acclaiming the Rock of our safety;
[2] let us come into his presence with thanksgiving,
   acclaiming him with music.

[3] For Yahweh is a great God,
   a greater King than all other gods;
[4] from depths of earth to mountain top
   everything comes under his rule;
[5] the sea belongs to him, he made it,
   so does the land, he shaped this too.

[6] Come in, let us bow, prostrate ourselves,
   and kneel in front of Yahweh our maker,
[7] for this is our God,
   and we are the people he pastures,
   the flock that he guides.

If only you would listen to him today,
[8] "Do not harden your hearts as at Meribah,
   as you did that day at Massah in the wilderness,
[9] when your ancestors challenged me, tested me,
   although they had seen what I could do.

[10] "For forty years that generation repelled me,
   until I said: How unreliable these people
   who refuse to grasp my ways!
[11] And so, in anger, I swore that not one
   would reach the place of rest I had for them."

let the fields exult and all that is in them, / let all the woodland trees cry out for joy,
(*Psalm 96:12*)

Psalm 96

[1] Sing Yahweh a new song!
Sing to Yahweh, all the earth!
[2] Sing to Yahweh, bless his name.

Proclaim his salvation day after day,
[3] tell of his glory among the nations,
tell his marvels to every people.

[4] Yahweh is great, loud must be his praise,
he is to be feared beyond all gods.
[5] Nothingness, all the gods of the nations.

Yahweh himself made the heavens,
[6] in his presence are splendor and majesty,
in his sanctuary power and beauty.

[7] Pay tribute to Yahweh, families of the peoples
tribute to Yahweh of glory and power,
[8] tribute to Yahweh of his name's due glory.

Bring out the offering, bear it before him,
[9] worship Yahweh in his sacred court,
tremble before him, all the earth!

[10] Say among the nations, "Yahweh is king!"
Firm has he made the world, and unshakable;
he will judge each nation with strict justice.

[11] Let the heavens be glad, let earth rejoice,
let the sea thunder and all that it holds,
[12] let the fields exult and all that is in them,
let all the woodland trees cry out for joy,

[13] at the presence of Yahweh, for he comes,
he comes to judge the earth,
to judge the world with justice
and the nations with his truth.

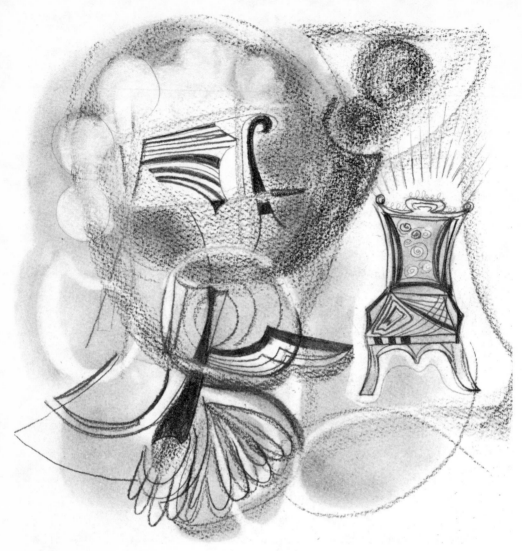

Cloud and Darkness surround him, / Righteousness and Justice support his throne.
(Psalm 97:2)

Psalm 97

[1] Yahweh is king! Let earth rejoice,
the many isles be glad!
[2] Cloud and Darkness surround him,
Righteousness and Justice support his throne.

[3] A fire precedes him as he goes,
devouring all enemies around him;
[4] his lightning lights up the world,
earth observes and quakes.

[5] The mountains melt like wax
at the coming of the Master of the world;
[6] the heavens proclaim his righteousness,
all nations see his glory.

[7] Shame on those who worship images,
who take pride in their idols:
bow down as he passes, all you gods!

[8] Zion hears and rejoices,
the daughters of Judah exult
at the rulings you utter, Yahweh.

[9] For you are Yahweh
Most High over the world,
far transcending all other gods.

[10] Yahweh loves those who repudiate evil,
he guards the souls of the devout,
rescuing them from the clutches of the wicked.

[11] Light dawns for the virtuous,
and joy, for upright hearts.
[12] Rejoice in Yahweh, you virtuous,
remember his holiness, and praise him!

Let the sea thunder and all that it holds, / and the world, with all who live in it;
(Psalm 98:7)

Psalm 98

Psalm

THE JUDGE OF THE WORLD

¹ Sing Yahweh a new song
   for he has performed marvels,
his own right hand, his holy arm,
   gives him the power to save.

² Yahweh has displayed his power;
  has revealed his righteousness to the nations,
³ mindful of his love and faithfulness
   to the house of Israel.

  The most distant parts of the earth have seen
   the saving power of our God.
⁴ Acclaim Yahweh, all the earth,
   burst into shouts of joy!

⁵ Sing to Yahweh, sing to the music of harps,
   and to the sound of many instruments;
⁶ to the sound of trumpet and horn
   acclaim Yahweh the King!

⁷ Let the sea thunder and all that it holds,
   and the world, with all who live in it;
⁸ let all the rivers clap their hands
   and the mountains shout for joy,

⁹ at the presence of Yahweh, for he comes
   to judge the earth,
  to judge the world with righteousness
   and the nations with strict justice.

Yahweh is king, the nations tremble; / he is enthroned on the cherubs, earth quakes;
(Psalm 99:1)

Psalm 99

GOD, RIGHTEOUS AND HOLY KING

¹ Yahweh is king, the nations tremble;
  he is enthroned on the cherubs, earth quakes;
²   Yahweh is great in Zion.

  He is high over all nations;
³ may they praise your great and terrible name,
⁴   "Holy is he, ·and mighty!"

  You are a king who loves justice,
  insisting on honesty, justice, virtue,
      as you have done for Jacob.

⁵   Let us extol Yahweh our God,
      and worship at his footstool,
          "Holy is he!"

⁶ Moses, Aaron one of his priests, and Samuel
  his votary, all invoked Yahweh:
      and he answered them.

⁷ He talked with them in the pillar of cloud;
  they obeyed his decrees, the Law he gave them.

⁸ Yahweh our God, you responded to them,
  a God of forgiveness for them,
      in spite of punishing their sins.

⁹ Extol Yahweh our God,
  worship at his holy mountain,
  "Holy is Yahweh our God!"

Walk through his porticoes giving thanks, / enter his courts praising
him, / give thanks to him, bless his name!
(Psalm 100:4)

Psalm 100

Psalm   For thanksgiving

INVITATION TO PRAISE GOD

[1] Acclaim Yahweh, all the earth,
[2] serve Yahweh gladly,
  come into his presence with songs of joy!

[3] Know that he, Yahweh, is God,
  he made us and we belong to him,
  we are his people, the flock that he pastures.

[4] Walk through his porticoes giving thanks,
  enter his courts praising him,
  give thanks to him, bless his name!

[5] Yes, Yahweh is good,
  his love is everlasting,
  his faithfulness endures from age to age.

There is no room in my house / for any hypocrite; / no liar keeps his post / where I can see him.
(*Psalm 101:7*)

Psalm 101

Of David   Psalm

THE IDEAL RULER

[1] My song is about kindness and justice;
Yahweh, I sing it to you.
[2] I mean to make good progress, as the blameless do:
when will you come to me?

In my household, I will advance
in purity of heart;
[3] I will not let my eyes rest
on any misconduct.

I hate the practices of the apostate,
they have no appeal for me;
[4] perverted hearts must keep their distance,
the wicked I disregard.

[5] The man who secretly slanders his neighbor
I reduce to silence;
haughty looks, proud heart,
I cannot tolerate these.

[6] I look to my religious countrymen
to compose my household;
only the man who makes progress, as the blameless do,
can be my servant.

[7] There is no room in my house
for any hypocrite;
no liar keeps his post
where I can see him.

[8] Morning after morning I reduce to silence
all who are wicked in this country,
banishing from the city of Yahweh
all evil men.

do not hide your face from me / when I am in trouble; / bend down to listen to me, / when I call, be quick to answer me!
(Psalm 102:2)

Psalm 102

Prayer of the downtrodden telling Yahweh their troubles at a moment of distress

PRAYER IN MISFORTUNE

1 Yahweh, hear my prayer,
   let my cry for help reach you;
2 do not hide your face from me
   when I am in trouble;
   bend down to listen to me,
   when I call, be quick to answer me!

3 For my days are vanishing like smoke,
   my bones smoldering like logs,
4 My heart shriveling like scorched grass
   and my appetite has gone;
5 whenever I heave a sigh,
   my bones stick through my skin.

6 I live in a desert like the pelican,
   in a ruin like the screech owl,
7 I stay awake, lamenting
   like a lone bird on the roof;
8 my enemies insult me all day long,
   those who used to praise me now use me as a curse.

9 Ashes are the bread I eat,
   what I drink I lace with tears,
10 under your furious anger,
   since you only picked me up to throw me down;
11 my days dwindle away like a shadow,
   I am as dry as hay.

12 Whereas, Yahweh, you remain for ever;
   each generation in turn remembers you!

13 Rise, take pity on Zion!—
   the time has come to have mercy on her,
   the hour has come;

14 for your servants prize her stones
   and are moved to pity by her dust.

15 Then will the nations fear the name of Yahweh
   and all kings on earth respect your glory;

¹⁶ when Yahweh builds Zion anew,
    he will be seen in his glory;
¹⁷ he will answer the prayer of the abandoned,
    he will not scorn their petitions.

¹⁸ Put this on record for the next generation,
    so that a race still to be born can praise God:
¹⁹ Yahweh has leaned down from the heights of his sanctuary,
    has looked down at earth from heaven,
²⁰ to hear the sighing of the captive,
    and to set free those doomed to die.

²⁸ Your servants' sons will have a permanent home,
    and their descendants be in your presence always,
²¹ to proclaim the name of Yahweh in Zion,
    his praise in Jerusalem;
²² nations and kingdoms will be united
    and offer worship to Yahweh together.

^{23a}   My strength has already run out;
^{24a}   tell me how much longer I have left.
^{24b}   Do not take me prematurely,
    when your own life lasts for ever.

²⁵   Aeons ago, you laid earth's foundations,
    the heavens are the work of your hands;
²⁶   all will vanish, though you remain,
    all wear out like a garment,
    like clothes that need changing you will change them;
²⁷   but yourself, you never change, and your years are unending.

in filling your years with prosperity, / in renewing your youth like an
eagle's.
(Psalm 103:5)

Psalm 103

Of David

GOD IS LOVE

[1] Bless Yahweh, my soul,
  bless his holy name, all that is in me!
[2] Bless Yahweh, my soul,
  and remember all his kindnesses:

[3] in forgiving all your offenses,
  in curing all your diseases,
[4] in redeeming your life from the Pit,
  in crowning you with love and tenderness,
[5] in filling your years with prosperity,
  in renewing your youth like an eagle's.
[6] Yahweh, who does what is right,
  is always on the side of the oppressed;
[7] he revealed his intentions to Moses,
  his prowess to the sons of Israel.

[8] Yahweh is tender and compassionate,
  slow to anger, most loving;
[9] his indignation does not last for ever,
  his resentment exists a short time only;
[10] he never treats us, never punishes us,
  as our guilt and our sins deserve.

[11] No less than the height of heaven over earth
  is the greatness of his love for those who fear him;
[12] he takes our sins farther away
  than the east is from the west.

[13] As tenderly as a father treats his children,
  so Yahweh treats those who fear him;
[14] he knows what we are made of,
  he remembers we are dust.

[15] Man lasts no longer than grass,
  no longer than a wild flower he lives,
[16] one gust of wind, and he is gone,
  never to be seen there again;

[17] yet Yahweh's love for those who fear him
  lasts from all eternity and for ever,
  like his goodness to their children's children,

[18] as long as they keep his covenant
and remember to obey his precepts.

[19] Yahweh has fixed his throne in the heavens,
his empire is over all.
[20] Bless Yahweh, all his angels,
heroes mighty to enforce his word,
attentive to his word of command.

[21] Bless Yahweh, all his armies,
servants to enforce his will.
[22] Bless Yahweh, all his creatures
in every part of his empire!

Bless Yahweh, my soul.

Psalm 104

[1] Bless Yahweh, my soul.
Yahweh my God, how great you are!
Clothed in majesty and glory,
[2] wrapped in a robe of light!

You stretch the heavens out like a tent,
[3] you build your palace on the waters above;
using the clouds as your chariot,
you advance on the wings of the wind;
[4] you use the winds as messengers
and fiery flames as servants.

[5] You fixed the earth on its foundations,
unshakable for ever and ever;
[6] you wrapped it with the deep as with a robe,
the waters overtopping the mountains.

[7] At your reproof the waters took to flight,
they fled at the sound of your thunder,
[8] cascading over the mountains, into the valleys,
down to the reservoir you made for them;
[9] you imposed the limits they must never cross again,
or they would once more flood the land.

[10] You set springs gushing in ravines,
running down between the mountains,
[11] supplying water for wild animals,
attracting the thirsty wild donkeys;
[12] near there the birds of the air make their nests
and sing among the branches.

[13] From your palace you water the uplands
until the ground has had all that your heavens have to offer;
[14] you make fresh grass grow for cattle
and those plants made use of by man,
for them to get food from the soil:
[15] wine to make them cheerful,
oil to make them happy
and bread to make them strong.

[16] The trees of Yahweh get rain enough,
those cedars of Lebanon he planted;

you build your palace on the waters above; / using the clouds as your chariot, / you advance on the wings of the wind;
(*Psalm 104:3*)

[17] here the little birds build their nest
and, on the highest branches, the stork has its home.
[18] For the wild goats there are the mountains,
in the crags rock badgers hide.

[19] You made the moon to tell the seasons,
the sun knows when to set:
[20] you bring darkness on, night falls,
all the forest animals come out:
[21] savage lions roaring for their prey,
claiming their food from God.

²² The sun rises, they retire,
   going back to lie down in their lairs,
²³ and man goes out to work,
   and to labor until dusk.
²⁴ Yahweh, what variety you have created,
   arranging everything so wisely!
   Earth is completely full of things you have made:

²⁵ among them vast expanse of ocean,
   teeming with countless creatures,
   creatures large and small,
²⁶ with the ships going to and fro
   and Leviathan whom you made to amuse you.

²⁷ All creatures depend on you
   to feed them throughout the year;
²⁸ you provide the food they eat,
   with generous hand you satisfy their hunger.

²⁹ You turn your face away, they suffer,
   you stop their breath, they die
   and revert to dust.
³⁰ You give breath, fresh life begins,
   you keep renewing the world.

³¹ Glory for ever to Yahweh!
   May Yahweh find joy in what he creates,
³² at whose glance the earth trembles,
   at whose touch the mountains smoke!

³³ I mean to sing to Yahweh all my life,
   I mean to play for my God as long as I live.
³⁴ May these reflections of mine give him pleasure,
   as much as Yahweh gives me!
³⁵ May sinners vanish from the earth
   and the wicked exist no more!

   Bless Yahweh, my soul.

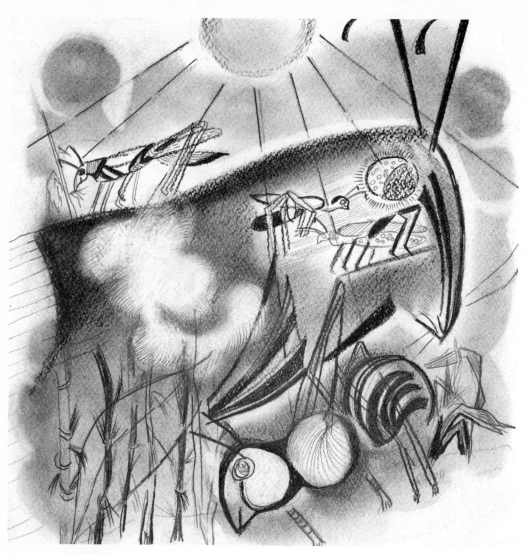

He spoke: there came locusts, / grasshoppers, more than you could count,
(Psalm 105:34)

Psalm 105

Alleluia!

1 Give thanks to Yahweh, call his name aloud,
  proclaim his deeds to the peoples!
2 Sing to him, play to him,
  tell over all his marvels!
3 Glory in his holy name,
  let the hearts that seek Yahweh rejoice!

4 Seek Yahweh and his strength,
  seek his face untiringly;
5 remember the marvels he has done,
  his wonders, the judgments from his mouth.

6 Stock of Abraham his servant,
  sons of Jacob his chosen one!
7 He is Yahweh our God,
  his authority is over all the earth.

8 Remember his covenant for ever,
  his word of command for a thousand generations,
9 the pact he made with Abraham,
  his oath to Isaac.

10 He established it as a statute for Jacob,
  an everlasting covenant for Israel.
11 "I give you a land," he said,
  "Canaan, your allotted heritage.

12 "There where you were easily counted,
  few in number, strangers to the country."
13 They went from nation to nation,
  from one kingdom to another people;

14 he let no man oppress them,
  he punished kings on their behalf.
15 "Do not touch my anointed ones," he said,
  "do not harm my prophets!"

16 Next, he called down famine on the country,
  he broke their staff, that is, their bread;
17 he sent a man ahead of them,
  Joseph, sold as a slave.

¹⁸ They tortured his feet with fetters,
   they put his neck in irons;
¹⁹ time passed, Joseph's oracle came true,
   Yahweh's word proved him right.

²⁰ The king gave orders to release him,
   that master of nations set him free,
²¹ putting him in charge of his household,
   in control of all he possessed,

²² to train his officials as he thought fit
   and convert his elders into sages.
²³ Israel then migrated to Egypt,
   Jacob settled in the land of Ham.

²⁴ He made his people fertile
   and more vigorous than their oppressors,
²⁵ whose hearts he then disposed to hatred of his people
   and double-dealing with his servants.

²⁶ He sent his servant Moses,
   and Aaron, the man of his choice;
²⁷ there they displayed his signs,
   his wonders in the land of Ham.

²⁸ He sent darkness, darkness fell,
   but still they defied his word.
²⁹ He turned their rivers into blood,
   thus killing all their fish.

³⁰ Their country was overrun with frogs
   even in the royal apartments;
³¹ he spoke: flies and mosquitoes
   swarmed throughout the country.

³² He sent them hail instead of rain,
   fire swept across their land;
³³ he blasted their vines and fig trees,
   he shattered the trees throughout the country.

³⁴ He spoke: there came locusts,
   grasshoppers, more than you could count,
³⁵ eating every scrap of greenstuff,
   every blade their soil produced.

³⁶ Next, he struck down all the first-born in their land,
   the entire first fruits of their fertility;
³⁷ then he led Israel out with gold and silver,
   and not one man of their tribes was left behind.

[38] Egypt was glad to see them go,
   they had filled her with alarm;
[39] he spread a cloud to cover them,
   and a fire to glow at night.

[40] They demanded food, he sent them quails,
   he satisfied them with the bread of heaven;
[41] he opened the rock, the waters gushed
   to flow through the desert like a river.

[42] Yes, faithful to the sacred promise
   given to his servant Abraham,
[43] he led his happy people forward,
   to joyful shouts from his chosen,

[44] and gave them the pagans' territories.
   Where others had toiled, they took possession,
[45] on condition that they kept his statutes
   and remained obedient to his laws.

Yahweh our God and savior, / gather us from among the pagans, / to give thanks to your holy name / and to find our happiness in praising you.
(*Psalm 106:47*)

Psalm 106

Alleluia!

1 Give thanks to Yahweh, for he is good,
  his love is everlasting!
2 Who can count all Yahweh's triumphs?
  Who can praise him enough?

3 Happy are we if we exercise justice
  and constantly practice virtue!
4 Yahweh, remember me,
  for the love you bear your people,
  come to me as a savior,
5 let me share the happiness of your chosen,
  the joys of your nation
  and take pride in being one of your heirs.

6 We have sinned quite as much as our fathers,
  we have been wicked, we are guilty;
7 our ancestors in Egypt never grasped
  the meaning of your marvels.

  They failed to appreciate your great love,
  they defied the Most High at the Sea of Reeds.
8 For the sake of his name, he saved them
  to demonstrate his power.

9 One word from him dried up the Sea of Reeds,
  he led them across the sea bed like dry land,
10 he saved them from the grasp of those who hated them
  and rescued them from the clutches of the enemy.

11 And the waters swallowed their oppressors,
  not one of them was left.
12 Then, having faith in his promises,
  they immediately sang his praises.

13 They forgot his achievements as quickly,
  going on before asking his advice;
14 their desires overcame them in the desert,
  they challenged God in the wilds.

15 He granted them what they asked for,
  then struck them with a wasting fever;

¹⁶ in camp, they grew jealous of Moses
   and Aaron, Yahweh's holy one.

¹⁷ The earth opened, swallowing Dathan,
   closing on Abiram's faction,
¹⁸ fire flamed out against their faction,
   the renegades went up in flames.

¹⁹ They made a calf at Horeb,
   performed prostrations to a smelted thing,
²⁰ exchanging the one who was their glory
   for the image of a grass-eating ox.

²¹ They forgot the God who had saved them
   by performing such feats in Egypt,
²² such wonders in the land of Ham,
   such fearful things at the Sea of Reeds.

²³ He talked of putting an end to them
   and would have done, if Moses his chosen
   had not stood in the breach, confronting him,
   and deflecting his destructive anger.

²⁴ They refused a land of delight,
   having no faith in his promise;
²⁵ they stayed in their camp and grumbled,
   they would not listen to Yahweh's voice.

²⁶ So, raising his hand, he swore
   to make them fall dead in the desert
²⁷ and their descendants to fall to the heathen,
   and to disperse them throughout those countries.

²⁸ They accepted the yoke of Baal-peor
   and ate sacrifices to the dead.
²⁹ They provoked him by their behavior;
   plague broke out among them.

³⁰ Then up stood Phinehas to intervene,
   and the plague was checked;
³¹ hence his reputation for virtue
   through successive generations for ever.

³² They enraged him at the waters of Meribah;
   as a result, things went wrong for Moses,
³³ since they had embittered his spirit
   and he spoke without stopping to think.

³⁴ They did not destroy the pagans
   as Yahweh had told them to do,

[35] but, intermarrying with them,
   adopted their practices instead.

[36] Serving the pagans' idols,
   they found themselves trapped
[37] into sacrificing their own sons
   and daughters to demons.

[38] They shed innocent blood,
   the blood of their sons and daughters,
   offering them to the idols of Canaan,
   they polluted the country with blood.

[39] They defiled themselves by such actions,
   their behavior was that of a whore.
[40] Yahweh's anger blazed out at his people,
   he came to loathe his heirs.

[41] He handed them over to the pagans,
   those who hated them became their masters;
[42] their enemies tyrannized over them,
   crushing them under their rule.

[43] Time and again he rescued them,
   but they went on defying him deliberately
   and plunging deeper into wickedness;
[44] even so, he took pity on their distress
   each time he heard them calling.

[45] For their sake, he remembered his covenant,
   he relented in his great love,
[46] making their captors mitigate
   the harshness of their treatment.

[47] Yahweh our God and savior,
   gather us from among the pagans,
   to give thanks to your holy name
   and to find our happiness in praising you.

[48] Blessed be Yahweh the God of Israel,
   from all eternity and for ever!
   Here, all the people are to say, "Amen."

who bent them double with hardship, / to breaking point, with no one to help them.
(Psalm 107:12)

Psalm 107

Alleluia!

¹ Give thanks to Yahweh, for he is good,
  his love is everlasting:

² let these be the words of Yahweh's redeemed,
  those he has redeemed from the oppressor's clutches,
³ by bringing them home from foreign countries,
  from east and west, from north and south.

⁴ Some had lost their way in the wilds and the desert,
  not knowing how to reach an inhabited town;
⁵ they were hungry and desperately thirsty,
  their courage was running low.

⁶ Then they called to Yahweh in their trouble
  and he rescued them from their sufferings,
⁷ guiding them by a route leading
  direct to an inhabited town.

⁸ Let these thank Yahweh for his love,
  for his marvels on behalf of men;
⁹ satisfying the hungry,
  he fills the starving with good things.

¹⁰ Some were living in gloom and darkness,
  fettered in misery and irons
¹¹ for defying the orders of God,
  for scorning the advice of the Most High;
¹² who bent them double with hardship,
  to breaking point, with no one to help them.

¹³ Then they called to Yahweh in their trouble
  and he rescued them from their sufferings;
¹⁴ releasing them from gloom and darkness,
  shattering their chains.

¹⁵ Let these thank Yahweh for his love,
  for his marvels on behalf of men;
¹⁶ breaking bronze gates open,
  he smashes iron bars.

¹⁷ Some, driven frantic by their sins,
  made miserable by their own guilt

¹⁸ and finding all food repugnant,
   were nearly at death's door.

¹⁹ Then they called to Yahweh in their trouble
   and he rescued them from their sufferings;
²⁰ sending his word and curing them,
   he snatched them from the Pit.

²¹ Let these thank Yahweh for his love,
   for his marvels on behalf of men.
²² Let them offer thanksgiving sacrifices
   and proclaim with shouts of joy what he has done.

²³ Others, taking ship and going to sea,
   were plying their business across the ocean;
²⁴ they too saw what Yahweh could do,
   what marvels on the deep!

²⁵ He spoke and raised a gale,
   lashing up towering waves.
²⁶ Flung to the sky, then plunged to the depths,
   they lost their nerve in the ordeal,
²⁷ staggering and reeling like drunkards
   with all their seamanship adrift.

²⁸ Then they called to Yahweh in their trouble
   and he rescued them from their sufferings,
²⁹ reducing the storm to a whisper
   until the waves grew quiet,
³⁰ bringing them, glad at the calm,
   safe to the port they were bound for.

³¹ Let these thank Yahweh for his love,
   for his marvels on behalf of men.
³² Let them extol him at the Great Assembly
   and praise him in the Council of Elders.

³³ Sometimes he turned rivers into desert,
   springs of water into arid ground,
³⁴ or a fertile country into salt flats,
   because the people living there were wicked.

³⁵ Or again, he turned a desert into sheets of water,
   and an arid country into flowing springs,
³⁶ where he gave the hungry a home
   in which to found a habitable town.

³⁷ There, they sow the fields and plant their vines,
   there, they show a profitable harvest.

[38] He blesses them, they grow in number,
he sees that their livestock does not decrease.

[39] Their numbers had fallen, they had grown weak
under pressure of disaster and hardship.
[40] Pouring his contempt upon the nobly born,
he left them to wander in a trackless waste.

[41] But now, he lifts the needy out of their misery,
and gives them a flock of new families;
[42] at the sight of which, upright hearts rejoice
and wickedness must hold its tongue.

[43] If you are wise, study these things
and realize how Yahweh shows his love.

With God among us, we shall fight like heroes, / he will trample on our enemies.
(Psalm 108:13)

Psalm 108

Song   Psalm   Of David

MORNING HYMN AND NATIONAL PRAYER

¹ My heart is ready, God
  —I mean to sing and play.
    Awake, my muse,
² awake, lyre and harp,
    I mean to wake the Dawn!

³ Yahweh, I mean to thank you among the peoples,
    to play music to you among the nations;
⁴ your love is high as heaven,
    your faithfulness as the clouds.
⁵ Rise high above the heavens, God,
    let your glory be over the earth!

⁶ To bring rescue to those you love
  save with your right hand and answer us!

⁷ God promised us once from his sanctuary,
    "I the Victor will parcel out Shechem,
    and share out the Valley of Succoth.

⁸ "Gilead is mine, Manasseh mine,
    Ephraim is my helmet,
    Judah, my marshal's baton.

⁹ "Moab a bowl for me to wash in!
    I throw my sandal over Edom
    and shout: Victory! over Philistia."

¹⁰ Who is there now to take me into the fortified city,
    to lead me into Edom?
¹¹ God, can you really have rejected us?
    You no longer march with our armies.

¹² Help us in this hour of crisis,
    the help that man can give is worthless.
¹³ With God among us, we shall fight like heroes,
    he will trample on our enemies.

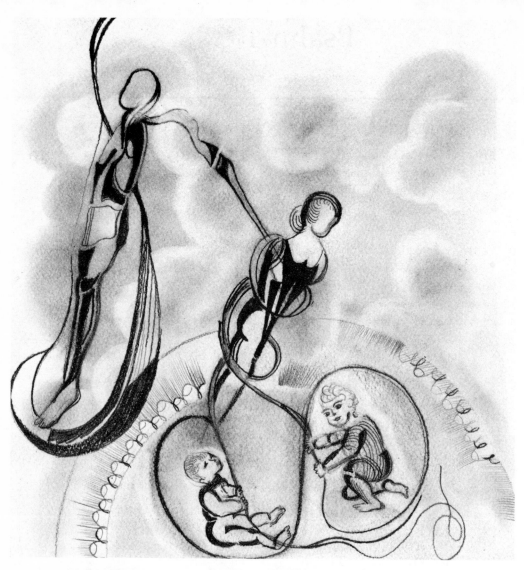

may his children be orphaned / and his wife widowed!
(*Psalm 109:9*)

Psalm 109

For the choirmaster   Of David   Psalm

AN APPEAL AGAINST ENEMIES

[1] God whom I praise, break your silence,
[2] now that the wicked and the false
    are both accusing me.
  They are defaming me,
[3] saying malicious things about me,
    attacking me for no reason.

[4] In return for my friendship, they denounce me,
    though all I had done was pray for them;
[5] they pay me back evil for kindness
    and hatred for friendship.

[6] "Give him a venal judge,
  find someone to frame the charge;
[7] let him be tried and found guilty,
  let his prayer be construed as a crime!

[8] "Let his life be cut short,
  let someone else take his office;
[9] may his children be orphaned
  and his wife widowed!

[10] "May his children be homeless vagabonds,
  beggared and hounded from their hovels;
[11] may the creditor seize his possessions
  and foreigners swallow his profits!

[12] "May no one be left to show him kindness,
  may no one look after his orphans,
[13] may his family die out,
  its name disappear in one generation!

[14] "May the crimes of his fathers be held against him
  and his mother's sin never be effaced;
[15] may Yahweh bear these constantly in mind,
  to wipe their memory off the earth!"

[16] That wretch never thought of being kind,
  but hounded the poor, the needy
  and the brokenhearted to death.
[17] He loved cursing, may it recoil on him,
  had no taste for blessing, may it shun him!

¹⁸ He used to wrap curses around him like a cloak,
  let them soak right into him like water,
  deep into his bones like oil.
¹⁹ May they now envelop him like a gown,
  be tied around his waist for ever!

²⁰ May Yahweh pay all my accusers,
  all my detractors like this!
²¹ Yahweh, defend me for the sake of your name,
  rescue me, since your love is generous!

²² Reduced to weakness and poverty,
  my heart is sorely tormented;
²³ I am dwindling away like a shadow,
  they have brushed me off like a locust.

²⁴ My knees are weak for lack of food,
  my body is thin for lack of oil;
²⁵ I have become an object of derision,
  people shake their heads at me in scorn.

²⁶ Help me, Yahweh my God,
  save me since you love me,
²⁷ and let them know that you have done it,
  that it was you, Yahweh, who did it.

²⁸ Counter their curses with your blessing,
  shame my aggressors, make your servant glad!
²⁹ Clothe my accusers in disgrace,
  cover them with a cloak of shame.

³⁰ I will give thanks aloud to Yahweh
  and praise him in the Assembly,
³¹ for conducting the poor man's defense
  against those who would have sentenced him to death.

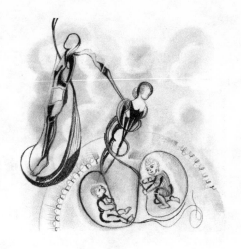

Drinking from the stream as he goes, / he can hold his head high in victory.
(*Psalm 110:7*)

Psalm 110

Of David   Psalm

[1] Yahweh's oracle to you, my Lord, "Sit at my right hand
and I will make your enemies a footstool for you."

[2] Yahweh will force all your enemies
under the sway of your scepter in Zion.

[3] Royal dignity was yours from the day you were born, on the holy
    mountains,
royal from the womb, from the dawn of your earliest days.

[4] Yahweh has sworn an oath which he never will retract,
"You are a priest of the order of Melchizedek, and for ever."

[5] The Lord is at your right hand.
When he grows angry he shatters kings,
[6] he gives the nations their deserts,
smashing their skulls, he heaps the wide world with corpses.
[7] Drinking from the stream as he goes,
he can hold his head high in victory.

The works of Yahweh are sublime, / those who delight in them are right to fix their eyes on them.
(*Psalm* 111:2)

Psalm 111

[1] Alleluia!

I give thanks to Yahweh with all my heart
where the virtuous meet and the people assemble.

[2] The works of Yahweh are sublime,
those who delight in them are right to fix their eyes on them.

[3] Every work that he does is full of glory and majesty,
and his righteousness can never change.

[4] He allows us to commemorate his marvels.
Yahweh is merciful and tenderhearted,

[5] he provides food for those who fear him;
he never forgets his covenant.

[6] He reminds his people of the power that he wields
by giving them the inheritance of the nations.

[7] All that he does is done in faithfulness and justice,
in all ways his precepts are dependable,

[8] ordained to last for ever and ever,
framed in faithfulness and integrity.

[9] Quickly he comes to his people's rescue,
imposing his covenant once and for all;
so holy his name, commanding our dread.

[10] This fear of Yahweh is the beginning of wisdom,
they have sound sense who practice it.
His praises will be sung for ever.

For the upright he shines like a lamp in the dark, / he is merciful, tenderhearted, virtuous.
(*Psalm 112:4*)

Psalm 112

IN PRAISE OF THE VIRTUOUS

[1] Alleluia!

Happy the man who fears Yahweh
by joyfully keeping his commandments!

[2] Children of such a man will be powers on earth,
descendants of the upright will always be blessed.

[3] There will be riches and wealth for his family,
and his righteousness can never change.

[4] For the upright he shines like a lamp in the dark,
he is merciful, tenderhearted, virtuous.

[5] Interest is not charged by this good man,
he is honest in all his dealings.

[6] Kept safe by virtue, he is ever steadfast,
and leaves an imperishable memory behind him;

[7] with constant heart, and confidence in Yahweh,
he need never fear bad news.

[8] Steadfast in heart he overcomes his fears:
in the end he will triumph over his enemies.

[9] Quick to be generous, he gives to the poor,
his righteousness can never change,
men such as this will always be honored,

[10] though this fills the wicked with fury
until, grinding their teeth, they waste away,
vanishing like their vain hopes.

Blessed be the name of Yahweh, / henceforth and for ever!
(*Psalm 113:2*)

Psalm 113

TO GOD THE GLORIOUS, THE MERCIFUL

[1] Alleluia!

You servants of Yahweh, praise,
praise the name of Yahweh!
[2] Blessed be the name of Yahweh,
henceforth and for ever!
[3] From east to west,
praised be the name of Yahweh!

[4] High over all nations, Yahweh!
His glory transcends the heavens!
[5] Who is like Yahweh our God?—
enthroned so high, he needs to stoop
[6] to see the sky and earth!

[7] He raises the poor from the dust;
he lifts the needy from the dunghill
[8] to give them a place with princes,
with the princes of his people.
[9] He enthrones the barren woman in her house
by making her the happy mother of sons.

Quake, earth, at the coming of your Master, / at the coming of the God of Jacob,
(Psalm 114:7)

Psalm 114

Alleluia!

1 When Israel came out of Egypt,
  the House of Jacob from a foreign nation,
2 Judah became his sanctuary
  and Israel his domain.

3 The sea fled at the sight,
  the Jordan stopped flowing,
4 the mountains skipped like rams,
  and like lambs, the hills.

5 Sea, what makes you run away?
  Jordan, why stop flowing?
6 Why skip like rams, you mountains,
  why like lambs, you hills?

7 Quake, earth, at the coming of your Master,
  at the coming of the God of Jacob,
8 who turns rock into pool,
  flint into fountain.

Psalm 115

[1] Not by us, Yahweh, not by us,
   by you alone is glory deserved,
   by your love and your faithfulness!
[2] Do the pagans ask, "Where is their God?"

[3] Ours is the God whose will is sovereign
   in the heavens and on earth,
[4] whereas their idols, in silver and gold,
   products of human skill,

[5] have mouths, but never speak,
   eyes, but never see,
[6] ears, but never hear,
   noses, but never smell,

[7] hands, but never touch,
   feet, but never walk,
   and not a sound from their throats.
[8] Their makers will end up like them,
   and so will anyone who relies on them.

[9] House of Israel, rely on Yahweh,
   on him, our help and shield!
[10] House of Aaron, rely on Yahweh,
   on him, our help and shield!
[11] You who fear Yahweh, rely on Yahweh,
   on him, our help and shield!

[12] Yahweh remembers us, he will bless,
   he will bless the House of Israel,
   he will bless the House of Aaron,
[13] he will bless those who fear Yahweh,
   without distinction of rank.

[14] May Yahweh add to your numbers,
   yours and your children's too!
[15] May you be blessed by Yahweh,
   maker of heaven and earth!
[16] Heaven belongs to Yahweh,
   earth he bestows on man.

whereas their idols, in silver and gold, / products of human skill,
(*Psalm 115:4*)

[17] The dead cannot praise Yahweh,
   they have gone down to silence;
[18] but we, the living, bless Yahweh
   henceforth and evermore.

Psalm 116

Alleluia!

¹ I love! For Yahweh listens
    to my entreaty;
² he bends down to listen to me
    when I call.

³ Death's cords were tightening around me,
    the nooses of Sheol;
distress and anguish gripped me,
⁴   I invoked the name of Yahweh:

"Yahweh, rescue me!"

⁵ Yahweh is righteous and merciful,
    our God is tenderhearted;
⁶ Yahweh defends the simple,
    he saved me when I was brought to my knees.

⁷ Return to your resting place, my soul,
    Yahweh has treated you kindly.
⁸ He has rescued (me from death) my eyes from tears
    and my feet from stumbling.

⁹ (I will walk in Yahweh's presence
    in the land of the living.)

¹⁰ I have faith, even when I say,
    "I am completely crushed."
¹¹ In my alarm, I declared,
    "No man can be relied on."

¹² What return can I make to Yahweh
    for all his goodness to me?
¹³ I will offer libations to my savior,
    invoking the name of Yahweh.

¹⁴ (I will pay what I vowed to Yahweh;
    may his whole nation be present!)

¹⁵ The death of the devout
    costs Yahweh dear.
¹⁶ Yahweh, I am your servant,
your servant, son of a pious mother,
    you undo my fetters.

(I will walk in Yahweh's presence / in the land of the living.)
(Psalm 116:9)

17 I will offer you the thanksgiving sacrifice,
   invoking the name of Yahweh.
9 I will walk in Yahweh's presence
   in the land of the living.

18 I will pay what I vowed to Yahweh;
   may his whole nation be present,
19 in the courts of the house of Yahweh,
   in your heart, Jerusalem.

Praise Yahweh, all nations, / extol him, all you peoples!
(*Psalm 117:1*)

Psalm 117

SUMMONS TO PRAISE

Alleluia!

[1] Praise Yahweh, all nations,
    extol him, all you peoples!
[2] For his love is strong,
    his faithfulness eternal.

I was pressed, pressed, about to fall, / but Yahweh came to my help;
(*Psalm 118:13*)

Psalm 118

Alleluia!

1 Give thanks to Yahweh, for he is good,
    his love is everlasting!
2 Let the House of Israel say it,
    "His love is everlasting!"

3 Let the House of Aaron say it,
    "His love is everlasting!"
4 Let those who fear Yahweh say it,
    "His love is everlasting!"

5 Hard pressed, I invoked Yahweh,
    he heard me and came to my relief.
6 With Yahweh on my side, I fear nothing:
    what can man do to me?
7 With Yahweh on my side, best help of all,
    I can triumph over my enemies.

8 I would rather take refuge in Yahweh
    than rely on men;
9 I would rather take refuge in Yahweh
    than rely on princes.

10 The pagans were swarming around me,
in the name of Yahweh I cut them down,
11 they swarmed around me closer and closer,
in the name of Yahweh I cut them down;

12 they swarmed around me like bees,
they blazed like a thorn fire,
in the name of Yahweh I cut them down.

13 I was pressed, pressed, about to fall,
    but Yahweh came to my help;
14 Yahweh is my strength and my song,
    he has been my savior.

15 Shouts of joy and safety
    in the tents of the virtuous:
Yahweh's right hand is wreaking havoc,
16   Yahweh's right hand is winning,
Yahweh's right hand is wreaking havoc!

[17] No, I shall not die, I shall live
   to recite the deeds of Yahweh;
[18] though Yahweh has punished me often,
   he has not abandoned me to Death.

[19] Open the gates of virtue to me,
   I will come in and give thanks to Yahweh.
[20] This is Yahweh's gateway,
   through which the virtuous may enter.
[21] I thank you for having heard me,
   you have been my savior.

[22] It was the stone rejected by the builders
   that proved to be the keystone;
[23] this is Yahweh's doing
   and it is wonderful to see.
[24] This is the day made memorable by Yahweh,
   what immense joy for us!

[25] Please, Yahweh, please save us.
   Please, Yahweh, please give us prosperity.
[26] Blessings on him who comes in the name of Yahweh!
   We bless you from the house of Yahweh.
[27] Yahweh is God, he smiles on us.
   With branches in your hands draw up in procession
   as far as the horns of the altar,

[28] You are my God, I give you thanks,
   I extol you, my God;
   I give you thanks for having heard me,
   you have been my savior.
[29] Give thanks to Yahweh, for he is good,
   his love is everlasting!

Exile though I am on earth, / do not hide your commandments from me.
(*Psalm 119:19*)

Psalm 119

1 Ah, how happy those of blameless life
who walk in the Law of Yahweh!
2 How happy those who respect his decrees,
and seek him with their whole heart,
3 and, doing no evil,
walk in his ways!
4 You yourself have made your precepts known,
to be faithfully kept.
5 Oh, may my behavior be constant
in keeping your statutes.
6 If I concentrate on your every commandment,
I can never be put to shame.
7 I thank you from an upright heart,
schooled in your rules of righteousness.
8 I mean to observe your statutes;
never abandon me.

9 How can a youth remain pure?
By behaving as your word prescribes.
10 I have sought you with all my heart,
do not let me stray from your commandments.
11 I have treasured your promises in my heart,
since I have no wish to sin against you.
12 How blessed are you, Yahweh!
Teach me your statutes!
13 With my lips I have repeated them,
all these rulings from your own mouth.
14 In the way of your decrees lies my joy,
a joy beyond all wealth.
15 I mean to meditate on your precepts
and to concentrate on your paths.
16 I find my delight in your statutes,
I do not forget your word.

17 Be good to your servant and I shall live,
I shall observe your word.
18 Open my eyes: I shall concentrate
on the marvels of your Law.
19 Exile though I am on earth,
do not hide your commandments from me.

20 My soul is overcome
    with an incessant longing for your rulings.
21 You reprove the arrogant, the accursed
    who stray from your commandments.
22 Avert their insults and contempt from me,
    since I respect your decrees.
23 Though princes put me on trial,
    your servant will meditate on your statutes,
24 since your decrees are my delight,
    your statutes are my counselors.

25 Down in the dust I lie prostrate:
    revive me as your word has guaranteed.
26 I admitted my behavior, you answered me,
    now teach me your statutes.
27 Explain to me how to keep your precepts,
    that I may meditate on your marvels.
28 I am sleepless with grief:
    raise me as your word has guaranteed.
29 Turn me from the path of delusion,
    grant me the grace of your Law.
30 I have chosen the way of fidelity,
    I have set my heart on your rulings.
31 I cling to your decrees:
    Yahweh, do not disappoint me.
32 I run the way of your commandments,
    since you have set me free.

33 Expound to me the way of your statutes, Yahweh,
    and I will always respect them.
34 Explain to me how to respect your Law
    and how to observe it wholeheartedly.
35 Guide me in the path of your commandments,
    since my delight is there.
36 Turn my heart to your decrees
    and away from getting money.
37 Avert my eyes from lingering on inanities,
    give me life by your word.
38 Keep your promise to your servant,
    so that others in turn may fear you.
39 Avert the insults that I fear,
    in the kindness of your rulings.
40 Look how I yearn for your precepts:
    give me life by your righteousness.

41 For, Yahweh, visited by your love
    and saving help, as you have promised,

42   I can find an answer to the insults,
      since I rely on your word.

43   Do not deprive me of that faithful word,
      since my hope has always lain in your rulings.

44   Let me observe your Law unfailingly
      for ever and ever.

45   So, having sought your precepts,
      I shall walk in all freedom.

46   I shall proclaim your decrees to kings
      without fear of disgrace.

47   Your commandments fill me with delight,
      I love them deeply.

48   I stretch out my hands to your beloved commandments,
      I meditate on your statutes.

49   Remember the word you pledged your servant,
      on which you have built my hope.

50   This has been my comfort in my suffering:
      that your promise gives me life.

51   Endlessly the arrogant have jeered at me,
      but I have not swerved from your Law.

52   Remembering your rulings in the past,
      Yahweh, I take comfort.

53   Fury grips me when I see the wicked
      abandoning your Law.

54   Where I live in exile,
      your statutes are psalms for me.

55   All night, Yahweh, I remember your name
      and observe your Law.

56   Surely it will count to my credit:
      that I respect your precepts.

57   Have I not said, Yahweh, that my task
      is to observe your words?

58   Wholeheartedly I now entreat you,
      take pity on me as you have promised!

59   After reflecting on my behavior,
      I turn my feet to your decrees.

60   Wasting no time, I hurry
      to observe your commandments.

61   Though the nooses of the wicked tighten around me,
      I do not forget your Law.

62   I get up at midnight to thank you
      for the righteousness of your rulings.

63   I am a friend to all who fear you
      and observe your precepts.

64 Yahweh, your love fills the earth:
     teach me your statutes.

65 In accordance with your word, Yahweh,
     you have been good to your servant.
66 Teach me good sense and knowledge,
     for I rely on your commandments.
67 In earlier days I had to suffer, I used to stray,
     but now I remember your promise.
68 You, so good and kind,
     teach me your statutes!
69 Though the arrogant tell foul lies about me,
     I wholeheartedly respect your precepts.
70 Their hearts are gross as fat,
     but my delight is in your Law.
71 It was good for me to have to suffer,
     the better to learn your statutes.
72 I put the Law you have given
     before all the gold and silver in the world.

73 Yahweh, my maker, my preserver,
     explain your commandments for me to learn.
74 Seeing me, those who fear you will be glad,
     since I put my hope in your word.
75 I know that your rulings are righteous, Yahweh,
     that you make me suffer out of faithfulness.
76 Now, please let your love comfort me,
     as you have promised your servant.
77 Treat me tenderly, and I shall live,
     since your Law is my delight.
78 Shame seize the arrogant who defame me,
     when I meditate on your precepts!
79 May those who fear you rally to me,
     all those familiar with your decrees!
80 Blameless in your statutes be my heart:
     no such shame therefore for me!

81 Keeping my hope in your word,
     I have worn myself out waiting for you to save me,
82 and have strained my eyes waiting for your promise:
     when, I want to know, will you console me?
83 Though smoked as dry as a wineskin,
     I do not forget your statutes.
84 How much longer has your servant to live,
     when will you condemn my persecutors?
85 The arrogant have dug pitfalls for me
     in defiance of your Law.

86 Your commandments epitomize faithfulness;
    when liars hound me, you must help me.
87 Though these wretches have almost done for me,
    I have never abandoned your precepts.
88 Lovingly intervene, give me life,
    and I will observe your decrees.

89 Lasting to eternity, your word,
    Yahweh, unchanging in the heavens:
90 your faithfulness lasts age after age;
    you founded the earth to endure.
91 Creation is maintained by your rulings,
    since all things are your servants.
92 Had your Law not been my delight
    I should have perished in my suffering.
93 I shall never forget your precepts;
    by these you have kept me alive.
94 I am yours, save me,
    since I study your precepts.
95 The wicked may hope to destroy me,
    but I am scrupulous about your decrees.
96 I have noticed limitations to all perfection,
    but your commandment has no limits at all.

97 Meditating all day on your Law,
    how I have come to love it!
98 By your commandment, ever mine,
    how much wiser you have made me than my enemies!
99 How much subtler than my teachers,
    through my meditating on your decrees!
100 How much more perceptive than the elders,
    as a result of my respecting your precepts!
101 I refrain my feet from every evil path,
    the better to observe your word.
102 I do not turn aside from your rulings,
    since you yourself teach me these.
103 Your promise, how sweet to my palate!
    Sweeter than honey to my mouth!
104 Your precepts endow me with perception;
    I hate all deceptive paths.

105 Now your word is a lamp to my feet,
    a light on my path.
106 I have sworn to observe, I shall maintain,
    your righteous rulings.
107 Yahweh, though my suffering is acute,
    revive me as your word has guaranteed.

108 Yahweh, accept the homage that I offer,
      teach me your rulings.
109 I would lay down my life at any moment,
      I have never yet forgotten your Law.
110 The wicked have tried to trap me,
      but I have never yet veered from your precepts.
111 Your decrees are my eternal heritage,
      they are the joy of my heart.
112 I devote myself to obeying your statutes—
      compensation enough for ever!

113 Odious, those whose allegiance is divided;
      I love your Law!
114 You, my refuge and shield,
      I put my hope in your word.
115 Away from me, you wicked people!
      I will respect the commandments of my God.
116 Support me as you have promised, and I shall live,
      do not disappoint me of my hope.
117 Uphold me, and I shall be safe
      with your statutes constantly before my eyes.
118 You spurn all who stray from your statutes,
      their notions being delusion.
119 You scour the wicked off the earth like rust;
      that is why I love your decrees.
120 My whole being trembles before you,
      your rulings fill me with fear.

121 Persevering in justice and virtue,
      must I now be abandoned to my oppressors?
122 Guarantor of your servant's well-being,
      forbid the arrogant to oppress me!
123 My eyes are worn out looking for your saving help,
      for your promise of righteousness to come.
124 Treat your servant lovingly,
      teach me your statutes.
125 I am your servant; if you will explain,
      I shall embrace your decrees.
126 Yahweh, now is the time to act,
      your Law is being broken.
127 Yes, I love your commandments
      more than gold, than purest gold.
128 Yes, I rule myself by all your precepts;
      I hate all deceptive paths.

129 Your decrees are so wonderful
      my soul cannot but respect them.

130 As your word unfolds, it gives light,
and the simple understand.
131 I open my mouth, panting
eagerly for your commandments.
132 Turn to me please, pity me,
as you should those who love your name.
133 Direct my steps as you have promised,
let evil win no power over me.
134 Rescue me from human oppression;
I will observe your precepts.
135 Treat your servant kindly,
teach me your statutes.
136 My eyes stream with tears,
because others disregard your Law.

137 Righteous, indeed, Yahweh!
And all your rulings correct!
138 The decrees you impose, how righteous,
how absolutely faithful!
139 Zeal for your house devours me,
since my oppressors forget your word.
140 But your promise is well tested,
and your servant holds it dear.
141 Puny and despised as I am,
I do not forget your precepts.
142 Your righteousness is eternal righteousness,
your Law holds true for ever.
143 Though distress and anguish grip me,
your commandments are my delight.
144 Eternally righteous, your decrees—
explain them to me, and I shall live.

145 Sincere, my call—Yahweh, answer me!
I will respect your statutes.
146 I invoke you, save me,
I will observe your decrees.
147 I am up before dawn to call for help,
I put my hope in your word.
148 I lie awake throughout the night,
to meditate on your promise.
149 In your love, Yahweh, listen to my voice,
let your rulings give me life.
150 My cruel persecutors are closing in,
how remote they are from your Law!
151 But, Yahweh, you are closer still
and all your commandments are true.

152 Long have I known that your decrees
    were founded to last for ever.

153 Take note of my suffering and rescue me,
    for I do not forget your Law.
154 Take up my cause, defend me,
    give me life as you have promised.
155 You will never save the wicked,
    if they do not study your statutes,
156 but many are your mercies to me, Yahweh,
    by your rulings give me life.
157 Many hound me and oppress me,
    but I do not swerve from your decrees.
158 The sight of these renegades disgusts me,
    they do not observe your promise;
159 but, Yahweh, see how I love your precepts,
    and lovingly give me life.
160 Faithfulness is the essence of your word,
    your righteous rulings hold good for ever.

161 Unjustifiably though princes hound me,
    your word is what fills me with dread.
162 I rejoice in your promise,
    like someone on finding a vast treasure.
163 I hate, I detest, delusion;
    your Law is what I love.
164 Seven times daily I praise you
    for your righteous rulings.
165 Universal peace for those who love your Law,
    no stumbling blocks for them!
166 Waiting for you, Yahweh, my savior,
    I fulfill your commandments.
167 My soul observes your decrees;
    these I wholly love.
168 I observe your precepts, your decrees;
    you know how I keep to your paths.

169 Yahweh, may my cry approach your presence;
    let your word endow me with perception!
170 May my entreaty reach your presence;
    rescue me as you have promised.
171 May my lips proclaim your praise,
    since you teach me your statutes.
172 May my tongue recite your promise,
    since all your commandments are righteous.
173 May your hand be there to help me,
    since I have chosen your precepts.

174 I long for you, Yahweh, my savior,
    your Law is my delight.
175 Long may my soul live to praise you,
    long be your rulings my help!
176 I am wandering like a lost sheep:
    come and look for your servant.

No, I have never forgotten your commandments.

Yahweh, save me from these lying lips / and these faithless tongues!
(*Psalm 120:2*)

Psalm 120

Song of Ascents

THE ENEMIES OF PEACE

[1] When I am in trouble, I call to
Yahweh, and he answers me.
[2] Yahweh, save me from these lying lips
and these faithless tongues!

[3] How will he pay back the false oath
of a faithless tongue?
[4] With war arrows hardened
over red-hot charcoal!

[5] This is worse than a life in Meshech,
or camping in Kedar!

[6] Too long have I lived
among people who hate peace,
[7] who, when I propose peace,
are all for war.

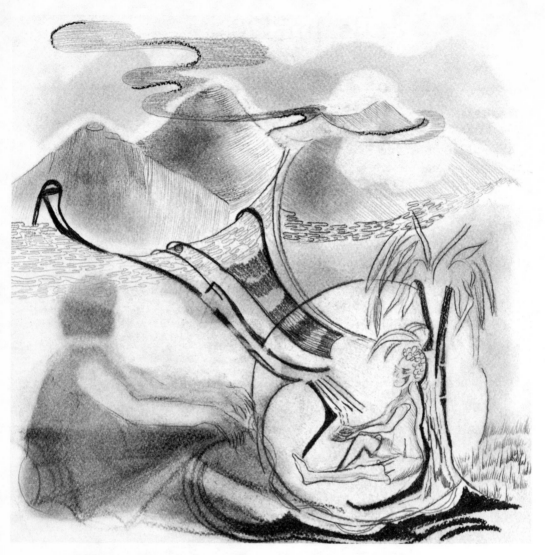

I lift my eyes to the mountains: / where is help to come from?
(*Psalm* 121:1)

Psalm 121

Song of Ascents

THE GUARDIAN OF ISRAEL

[1] I lift my eyes to the mountains:
   where is help to come from?
[2] Help comes to me from Yahweh,
   who made heaven and earth.

[3] No letting our footsteps slip!
   This guard of yours, he does not doze!
[4] The guardian of Israel
   does not doze or sleep.

[5] Yahweh guards you, shades you.
   With Yahweh at your right hand
[6] sun cannot strike you down by day,
   nor moon at night.

[7] Yahweh guards you from harm,
   he guards your lives,
[8] he guards you leaving, coming back,
   now and for always.

Jerusalem restored! The city, / one united whole!
(*Psalm 122:3*)

Psalm 122

Song of Ascents   Of David

HAIL, JERUSALEM!

[1] How I rejoiced when they said to me,
  "Let us go to the house of Yahweh!"
[2] And now our feet are standing
  in your gateways, Jerusalem.

[3] Jerusalem restored! The city,
  one united whole!
[4] Here the tribes come up,
  the tribes of Yahweh,

they come to praise Yahweh's name,
  as he ordered Israel,
[5] here where the tribunals of justice are,
  the royal tribunals of David.

[6] Pray for peace in Jerusalem,
  "Prosperity to your houses!
[7] Peace inside your city walls!
  Prosperity to your palaces!"

[8] Since all are my brothers and friends,
  I say "Peace be with you!"
[9] Since Yahweh our God lives here,
  I pray for your happiness.

eyes like the eyes of slaves / fixed on their master's hand; / like the eyes of a slave girl / fixed on the hand of her mistress, / so our eyes are fixed on Yahweh our God, / for him to take pity on us;
(*Psalm 123:2*)

Psalm 123

Song of Ascents

PRAYER OF THE DISTRESSED

[1] I lift my eyes to you,
    to you who have your home in heaven,
[2] eyes like the eyes of slaves
    fixed on their master's hand;

 like the eyes of a slave girl
    fixed on the hand of her mistress,
so our eyes are fixed on Yahweh our God,
    for him to take pity on us;

[3] pity us, Yahweh, take pity on us,
    we have had more than our share of scorn,
[4] more than our share
    of jeers from the complacent,
    of scorn from the proud.

who let us escape like birds / from the fowler's net. / He tore the net / and we escaped;
(*Psalm* 124:7)

Psalm 124

Song of Ascents   David

THE SAVIOR OF ISRAEL

[1] If Yahweh had not been on our side
   —let Israel repeat it—
[2] if Yahweh had not been on our side
   when they attacked us,
[3] they would have swallowed us alive
   and burned us to death in their rage.

[4] The waters would have closed over us,
   the torrent have swept us away,
[5] either would have drowned us
   in their turbulent waves.

[6] Blessed be Yahweh who did not let us fall
   a victim to those teeth,
[7] who let us escape like birds
   from the fowler's net.

He tore the net
   and we escaped;
[8] our help is in the name of Yahweh,
   who made heaven and earth.

Jerusalem! Encircled by mountains, / as Yahweh encircles his people / now and for always.
(*Psalm 125:2*)

Psalm 125

Song of Ascents

GOD PROTECTS HIS FAITHFUL

[1] Those who trust in Yahweh are like Mount Zion,
    unshakable, standing for ever.
[2] Jerusalem! Encircled by mountains,
  as Yahweh encircles his people
    now and for always.

[3] No wicked scepter shall rule
    this heritage of the virtuous,
  or the virtuous in their turn
    might take to evil.

[4] Yahweh, be good to the good,
    to those of upright heart.
[5] But the perverts, those who follow twisting paths—
    may Yahweh send them to join the evildoers!

  Peace to Israel!

They went away, went away weeping, / carrying the seed; / they come back, come back singing, / carrying their sheaves.
(Psalm 126:6)

Psalm 126

Song of Ascents

SONG OF THE RETURNING EXILES

[1] When Yahweh brought Zion's captives home,
　　at first it seemed like a dream;
[2] then our mouths filled with laughter
　　and our lips with song.

Even the pagans started talking
　　about the marvels Yahweh had done for us!
[3] What marvels indeed he did for us,
　　and how overjoyed we were!

[4] Yahweh, bring all our captives back again
　　like torrents in the Negeb!
[5] Those who went sowing in tears
　　now sing as they reap.

[6] They went away, went away weeping,
　　carrying the seed;
they come back, come back singing,
　　carrying their sheaves.

If Yahweh does not build the house, / in vain the masons toil; / if Yahweh does not guard the city, / in vain the sentries watch.
(*Psalm 127:1*)

Psalm 127

Song of Ascents   Solomon

TRUST IN PROVIDENCE

¹ If Yahweh does not build the house,
    in vain the masons toil;
  if Yahweh does not guard the city,
    in vain the sentries watch.

² In vain you get up earlier,
  and put off going to bed,
  sweating to make a living,
  since he provides for his beloved as they sleep.

³ Sons are a bounty from Yahweh,
  he rewards with descendants:
⁴ like the arrows in a hero's hand
  are the sons you father when young.

⁵ Happy the man who has filled his quiver
  with arrows of this sort;
  in dispute with his enemies at the gate,
  he will not be worsted.

Happy, all those who fear Yahweh / and follow in his paths.
(Psalm 128:1)

Psalm 128

Song of Ascents

BLESSING FOR THE DEVOUT

1 Happy, all those who fear Yahweh
and follow in his paths.

2 You will eat what your hands have worked for,
happiness and prosperity will be yours.
3 Your wife: a fruitful vine
on the inner walls of your house.
Your sons: around your table
like shoots around an olive tree.

4 Such are the blessings that fall
on the man who fears Yahweh.
5a May Yahweh bless you from Zion,
5c all the days of your life!
5b May you see Jerusalem prosperous
6 and live to see your children's children!

Peace to Israel!

May they all be thrown into confusion, be routed,/who have hated
Zion,
(Psalm 129:5)

Psalm 129

AGAINST THE ENEMIES OF ZION

[1] Hard as they have harried me since I was young
   —let Israel repeat it—
[2] hard as they have harried me since I was young,
   they have not overcome me.

[3] Plowmen have plowed on my back
   longer and longer furrows,
[4] but now Yahweh the Righteous has shattered
   the yoke of the wicked.

[5] May they all be thrown into confusion, be routed,
   who have hated Zion,
[6] be blasted by winds from the east like grass
   sprouting on the roof!

[7] Roof grass never yet filled
   reaper's arm or binder's lap—
[8] and no one passing them will ever say,
   "Yahweh's blessing on you!"

We bless you in the name of Yahweh.

Lord, listen to my cry for help! / Listen compassionately / to my pleading!
(Psalm 130:2)

Psalm 130

Song of Ascents

FROM THE DEPTHS

[1] From the depths I call to you, Yahweh,
[2] Lord, listen to my cry for help!
 Listen compassionately
   to my pleading!

[3] If you never overlooked our sins, Yahweh,
 Lord, could anyone survive?
[4] But you do forgive us:
   and for that we revere you.

[5] I wait for Yahweh, my soul waits for him,
   I rely on his promise,
[6]   my soul relies on the Lord
   more than a watchman on the coming of dawn.

[7] Let Israel rely on Yahweh
   as much as the watchman on the dawn!
 For it is with Yahweh that mercy is to be found,
 and a generous redemption;
[8] it is he who redeems Israel
   from all their sins.

Enough for me to keep my soul tranquil and quiet / like a child in its mother's arms, / as content as a child that has been weaned. (Psalm 131:2)

Psalm 131

Song of Ascents Of David

CHILDLIKE TRUST IN GOD

[1] Yahweh, my heart has no lofty ambitions,
   my eyes do not look too high.
 I am not concerned with great affairs
   or marvels beyond my scope.
[2] Enough for me to keep my soul tranquil and quiet
   like a child in its mother's arms,
 as content as a child that has been weaned.

[3] Israel, rely on Yahweh,
   now and for always!

Psalm 132

Song of Ascents

THE ARK IS TAKEN TO ZION: ANNIVERSARY HYMN

[1] Yahweh, remember David
  and all the hardships he suffered,
[2] and the oath he swore to Yahweh,
  his vow to the Mighty One of Jacob:

[3] not to enter tent or house,
  not to climb into bed,
[4] not to allow himself to sleep,
  not even to close his eyes,
[5] until he had found a place for Yahweh,
  a home for the Mighty One of Jacob!

[6] Listen: we heard it was in Ephrathah,
  we found it at Fields-of-the-Forest!
[7] Let us go where he is waiting
  and worship at his footstool.

[8] Yahweh, go up to your resting place,
  you and your ark of power.
[9] Your priests are vesting in virtue
  and your devout are shouting for joy.
[10] For the sake of your servant David,
  do not banish your anointed.

[11] Yahweh swore to David
  and will remain true to his word,
  "I promise that your own son
  shall succeed you on the throne.

[12] "If your sons observe my covenant,
  the decrees that I have taught them,
  their sons too shall succeed you
  on the throne for evermore."

[13] For Yahweh has chosen Zion,
  desiring this to be his home,
[14] "Here I will stay for ever,
  this is the home I have chosen.

[15] "I will bless her virtuous with riches,
  provide her poor with food,

Listen: we heard it was in Ephrathah, / we found it at Fields-of-the-Forest!
(*Psalm 132:6*)

¹⁶ vest her priests in salvation
  and her devout shall shout for joy.

¹⁷ "Here I will make a horn sprout for David,
  here, I will trim a lamp for my anointed,
¹⁸ whose enemies I shall clothe in shame,
  while his crown bursts into flower."

How good, how delightful it is / for all to live together like brothers:
(Psalm 133:1)

Psalm 133

Song of Ascents   Of David

BROTHERLY LOVE

[1] How good, how delightful it is
   for all to live together like brothers:

[2] fine as oil on the head,
   running down the beard,
 running down Aaron's beard
   to the collar of his robes;

[3] copious as a Hermon dew
   falling on the heights of Zion,
 where Yahweh confers his blessing,
   everlasting life.

Stretch out your hands toward the sanctuary, / bless Yahweh night after night!
(Psalm 134:2)

Psalm 134

Song of Ascents

NIGHT HYMN

[1] Come, bless Yahweh,
all you who serve Yahweh,
serving in the house of Yahweh,
in the courts of the house of our God!

[2] Stretch out your hands toward the sanctuary,
bless Yahweh night after night!

[3] May Yahweh bless you from Zion,
he who made heaven and earth!

I have learned for myself that Yahweh is great, / that our Lord surpasses all other gods.
(*Psalm 135:5*)

Psalm 135

[1] Alleluia!

Praise the name of Yahweh,
  praise Yahweh, you who serve him,
[2] serving in the house of Yahweh,
  in the courts of the house of our God!

[3] Praise Yahweh, for Yahweh is good.
  Play for his name, for he inspires love;
[4] since Yahweh has chosen Jacob,
  Israel as his own.

[5] I have learned for myself that Yahweh is great,
  that our Lord surpasses all other gods.
[6] In the heavens, on the earth,
  in the ocean, in the depths,
  Yahweh's will is sovereign.

[7] He raises up clouds from the boundaries of earth,
  makes the lightning flash for the downpour
  and brings the wind out of his storehouse.

[8] He struck down the first-born of Egypt,
  of man and beast alike,
[9] he sent signs and wonders
  among you, Egypt,
  against Pharaoh and his officials.

[10] He struck the pagans down in droves,
  he slaughtered mighty kings,
[11] Sihon, king of the Amorites,
  and Og, the king of Bashan,
  and all the kingdoms of Canaan;
[12] he gave their lands as a legacy,
  a legacy to his people Israel.

[13] Yahweh, your name endures for ever!
  Yahweh, your memory is always fresh!
[14] Since Yahweh vindicates his people,
  and cares for those who serve him;

[15] whereas pagans' idols, in silver and gold,
  products of human skill,

[16] have mouths, but never speak,
   eyes, but never see,

[17] ears, but never hear,
   and not a breath in their mouths.
[18] Their makers will end up like them
   and so will anyone who relies on them.

[19] House of Israel, bless Yahweh,
   House of Aaron, bless Yahweh,
[20] House of Levi, bless Yahweh,
   you who fear Yahweh, bless Yahweh!

[21] Blessed be Yahweh in Zion,
   in Jerusalem his home!

He provides for all living creatures, / his love is everlasting!
(*Psalm 136:25*)

Psalm 136

Alleluia!

[1] Give thanks to Yahweh, for he is good,
    his love is everlasting!
[2] Give thanks to the God of gods,
    his love is everlasting!
[3] Give thanks to the Lord of lords,
    his love is everlasting!

[4] He alone performs great marvels,
    his love is everlasting!
[5] His wisdom made the heavens,
    his love is everlasting!
[6] He set the earth on the waters,
    his love is everlasting!

[7] He made the great lights,
    his love is everlasting!
[8] The sun to govern the day,
    his love is everlasting!
[9] Moon and stars to govern the night,
    his love is everlasting!

[10] He struck down the first-born of Egypt,
    his love is everlasting!
[11] And brought Israel out,
    his love is everlasting!
[12] with mighty hand and outstretched arm,
    his love is everlasting!

[13] He split the Sea of Reeds,
    his love is everlasting!
[14] Led Israel through the middle,
    his love is everlasting!
[15] Drowned Pharaoh and his army,
    his love is everlasting!

[16] He led his people through the wilderness,
    his love is everlasting!
[17] He struck down mighty kings,
    his love is everlasting!

[18] He slaughtered famous kings,
   his love is everlasting!
[19] Sihon, king of the Amorites,
   his love is everlasting!
[20] And Og, the king of Bashan,
   his love is everlasting!

[21] He gave their lands as a legacy,
   his love is everlasting!
[22] A legacy to his servant Israel,
   his love is everlasting!
[23] He remembered us when we were down,
   his love is everlasting!
[24] And snatched us from our oppressors,
   his love is everlasting!

[25] He provides for all living creatures,
   his love is everlasting!
[26] Give thanks to the God of Heaven,
   his love is everlasting!

Beside the streams of Babylon / we sat and wept / at the memory of Zion,
(*Psalm 137:1*)

Psalm 137

BALLAD OF THE EXILES

[1] Beside the streams of Babylon
  we sat and wept
  at the memory of Zion,
[2] leaving our harps
  hanging on the poplars there.

[3] For we had been asked
  to sing to our captors,
  to entertain those who had carried us off:
  "Sing," they said,
  "some hymns of Zion."

[4] How could we sing
  one of Yahweh's hymns
  in a pagan country?
[5] Jerusalem, if I forget you,
  may my right hand wither!

[6] May I never speak again,
  if I forget you!
  If I do not count Jerusalem
  the greatest of my joys!

[7] Yahweh, remember
  what the Sons of Edom did
  on the day of Jerusalem,
  how they said, "Down with her!
  Raze her to the ground!"

[8] Destructive Daughter of Babel,
  a blessing on the man who treats you
  as you have treated us,
[9] a blessing on him who takes and dashes
  your babies against the rock!

I thank you, Yahweh, with all my heart, / because you have heard what I said. / In the presence of the angels I play for you,
(Psalm 138:1)

Psalm 138

Of David

HYMN OF THANKSGIVING

[1] I thank you, Yahweh, with all my heart,
because you have heard what I said.
In the presence of the angels I play for you,
[2] and bow down toward your holy Temple.

I give thanks to your name for your love and faithfulness;
your promise is even greater than your fame.
[3] The day I called for help, you heard me
and you increased my strength.

[4] Yahweh, all kings on earth give thanks to you,
for they have heard your promises;
[5] they celebrate Yahweh's actions,
"Great is the glory of Yahweh!"
[6] From far above, Yahweh sees the humble,
from far away he marks down the arrogant.

[7] Though I live surrounded by trouble,
you keep me alive—to my enemies' fury!
You stretch your hand out and save me,
[8] your right hand ·will do everything for me.
Yahweh, your love is everlasting,
do not abandon us whom you have made.

*your hand would still be guiding me, / your right hand holding me.
(Psalm 139:10)*

Psalm 139

For the choirmaster Of David Psalm

IN PRAISE OF GOD'S OMNISCIENCE

[1] Yahweh, you examine me and know me,
[2] you know if I am standing or sitting,
   you read my thoughts from far away,
[3] whether I walk or lie down, you are watching,
   you know every detail of my conduct.

[4] The word is not even on my tongue,
   Yahweh, before you know all about it;
[5] close behind and close in front you fence me around,
   shielding me with your hand.
[6] Such knowledge is beyond my understanding,
   a height to which my mind cannot attain.

[7] Where could I go to escape your spirit?
   Where could I flee from your presence?
[8] If I climb the heavens, you are there,
   there too, if I lie in Sheol.

[9] If I flew to the point of the sunrise,
   or westward across the sea,
[10] your hand would still be guiding me,
   your right hand holding me.

[11] If I asked darkness to cover me,
   and light to become night around me,
[12] that darkness would not be dark to you,
   night would be as light as day.

[13] It was you who created my inmost self,
   and put me together in my mother's womb;
[14] for all these mysteries I thank you:
   for the wonder of myself, for the wonder of your works.

   You know me through and through,
[15] from having watched my bones take shape
   when I was being formed in secret,
   knitted together in the limbo of the womb.

[16] You had scrutinized my every action,
   all were recorded in your book,
   my days listed and determined,
[17] even before the first of them ·occurred.

God, how hard it is to grasp your thoughts!
How impossible to count them!
[18] I could no more count them than I could the sand,
and suppose I could, you would still be with me.

[19] God, if only you would kill the wicked!
Men of blood, away from me!
[20] They talk blasphemously about you,
regard your thoughts as nothing.

[21] Yahweh, do I not hate those who hate you,
and loathe those who defy you?
[22] I hate them with a total hatred,
I regard them as my own enemies.

[23] God, examine me and know my heart,
probe me and know my thoughts;
[24] make sure I do not follow pernicious ways,
and guide me in the way that is everlasting.

Yahweh, guard me from attacks by the wicked, / defend me from those who love force, / from people plotting to make me stumble,
(*Psalm 140:4*)

Psalm 140

For the choirmaster   Psalm   Of David

AGAINST THE WICKED

1 Yahweh, rescue me from evil people,
    defend me from men of violence,
2 from people plotting evil,
    forever intent on stirring up strife,
3 who make their tongues as sharp as serpents'
    with viper's venom on their lips.   *Pause*

4 Yahweh, guard me from attacks by the wicked,
    defend me from those who love force,
  from people plotting to make me stumble,
5b   forever laying snares where I walk,
5a insolent wretches, concealing pitfall and noose
5b   to trap me as I pass.   *Pause*

6 I have told Yahweh, "You are my God."
    Yahweh, listen to my cry for help.
7 Yahweh, my Lord, my saving strength,
    shielding my head when I have to fight,
8 Yahweh, do not grant their wicked wishes,
    do not let their plots succeed.

9 May those besieging me not win.   *Pause*
    may their own cruel words overtake them,
10 may red-hot embers rain down on them,
    may they be flung into the abyss for good,
11 may evil hound the man of violence to death
    and the slanderer not hold his own on earth.

12 I know Yahweh will avenge the wretched,
    and see justice done for the poor.
13 The virtuous shall have good cause to thank your name,
    and the upright to find a home with you.

To you, Yahweh my Lord, I turn my eyes. / I take shelter in you, do not leave me exposed!
(Psalm 141:8)

Psalm 141

Psalm   Of David

AGAINST THE ATTRACTIONS OF EVIL

[1] Yahweh, I am calling, hurry to me,
   listen to me, I am invoking you.
[2] My prayers rise like incense,
   my hands like the evening offering.

[3] Yahweh, set a guard at my mouth,
   a watcher at the gate of my lips.
[4] Let me feel no impulse to do wrong,
   to share the godlessness of evildoers.

 No, I will not sample their delights.
[5] A virtuous man may strike me in reproof, for my own good,
   but a wicked one shall never anoint my head with oil!
   Daily I counter their malice with prayer.
[6] When their judges are flung on jagged rock,
   they will learn how mild my words have been,
[7] "Like a millstone smashed on the ground,
   our bones are scattered at the mouth of Sheol."

[8] To you, Yahweh my Lord, I turn my eyes.
   I take shelter in you, do not leave me exposed!
[9] Keep me out of traps that are set for me,
   from the bait laid for me by evil men.
[10] Let the wicked fall into their own net,
   while I go on my way.

my spirit fails me, / but you, you know my path. / On the path I
follow / they have concealed a trap.
(*Psalm 142:3*)

Psalm 142

Poem   Of David   When he was in the cave   Psalm

PRAYER OF A HUNTED MAN

[1] To Yahweh, my cry! I plead.
To Yahweh, my cry! I entreat.
[2] I pour out my supplications,
I unfold all my troubles;
[3] my spirit fails me,
but you, you know my path.

On the path I follow
they have concealed a trap.
[4] Look on my right and see,
there is no one to befriend me.
All help is denied me,
no one cares about me.

[5] I invoke you, Yahweh,
I affirm that you are my refuge,
my heritage in the land of the living.
[6] Listen to my cries for help,
I can hardly be crushed lower.

Rescue me from persecutors
stronger than I am!
[7] Free me from this imprisonment,
and I will thank your name once more
in the Assembly of the virtuous,
for the goodness you show me.

I stretch out my hands, / like thirsty ground I yearn for you.
(*Psalm 143:6*)

Psalm 143

Psalm   Of David

A HUMBLE ENTREATY

1 Yahweh, hear my prayer,
  listen to my pleading,
  answer me faithfully, righteously;
2 do not put your servant on trial,
  no one is virtuous by your standards.

3 An enemy who hounds me
  to crush me into the dust,
  forces me to dwell in darkness
  like the dead of long ago;
4 my spirit fails me
  and my heart is full of fear.

5 I recall the days of old,
  I reflect on all that you did,
  I ponder your deeds;
6 I stretch out my hands,
  like thirsty ground I yearn for you.   *Pause*

7 Quick, Yahweh, answer me
  before my spirit fails;
  if you hide your face much longer,
  I shall go down to the Pit like the rest.

8 Let dawn bring proof of your love,
  for one who relies on you;
  let it show the right road,
  to one who lifts up his soul to you.

9 Yahweh, rescue me from my enemies,
  I have fled to you for shelter;
10 teach me to obey you,
  since you are my God;
  may your good spirit guide me
  on to level ground.

11 Yahweh, for the sake of your name,
  keep your promise to save me;
  protect me from oppression,
12 love me, kill my enemies,
  destroy my oppressors,
  for I am your servant.

Psalm 144

David

WAR HYMN AND THE FRUITS OF VICTORY

¹ Blessed be Yahweh, my rock,
who trains my hands for war
and my fingers for battle,
² my love, my bastion,
my citadel, my savior,
I shelter behind him, my shield,
he makes the nations submit to me.

³ Yahweh, what is man, that you should notice him?
A human being, that you should think about him?
⁴ Man's life, a mere puff of wind,
his days, as fugitive as shadows.

⁵ Yahweh, lower your heavens, come down to us!
Touch the mountains, make them smoke,
⁶ flash your lightning—scatter them,
shoot your arrows—rout them.

⁷ Reach down your hand from above,
save me, rescue me from deep waters,
from the power of aliens
⁸ who tell nothing but lies,
who are prepared to swear to falsehood!

⁹ God, I have made a new song for you
to be played on the ten-string lyre,
¹⁰ you who give victory to kings
and safety to your servant David.

¹¹ From peril of sword ·save me,
rescue me from the power of aliens
who tell nothing but lies,
who are prepared to swear to falsehood!

¹² May our sons be like plants
growing strong from their earliest days,
our daughters like corner statues,
carvings fit for a palace;
¹³ may our barns overflow
with every possible crop,

May our sons be like plants / growing strong from their earliest days, / our daughters like corner-statues, / carvings fit for a palace;
(*Psalm 144:12*)

may the sheep in our fields be counted
    in their thousands and tens of thousands,
[14] may our cattle be stout and strong;
    and may there be an end of raids and exile,
and of panic in our streets.

[15] Happy the nation of whom this is true,
    happy the nation whose God is Yahweh!

Psalm 145

Hymn   Of David

HYMN OF PRAISE TO YAHWEH THE KING

¹ I sing your praises, God my King,
  I bless your name for ever and ever,
² blessing you day after day,
  and praising your name for ever and ever.
³ Can anyone measure the magnificence
  of Yahweh the great, and his inexpressible grandeur?

⁴ Celebrating your acts of power,
  one age shall praise your doings to another.
⁵ Oh, the splendor of your glory, your renown!
  I tell myself the story of your marvelous deeds.

⁶ Men will proclaim your fearful power
  and I shall assert your greatness;
⁷ they will celebrate your generous kindness
  and joyfully acclaim your righteousness.

⁸ He, Yahweh, is merciful, tenderhearted,
  slow to anger, very loving,
⁹ and universally kind; Yahweh's tenderness
  embraces all his creatures.

¹⁰ Yahweh, all your creatures thank you,
  and your faithful bless you.
¹¹ Kingly and glorious they proclaim you,
  they affirm your might.

¹² Let mankind learn your acts of power,
  and the majestic glory of your sovereignty!
¹³ Your sovereignty is an eternal sovereignty,
  your empire lasts from age to age.

  Always true to his promises,
  Yahweh shows love in all he does.
¹⁴ Only stumble, and Yahweh at once supports you,
  if others bow you down, he will raise you up.

¹⁵ Patiently all creatures look to you
  to feed them throughout the year;
¹⁶ quick to satisfy every need,
  you feed them all with a generous hand.

Your sovereignty is an eternal sovereignty, / your empire lasts from age to age. / Always true to his promises, / Yahweh shows love in all he does. (Psalm 145:13)

[17] Righteous in all that he does,
Yahweh acts only out of love,
[18] standing close to all who invoke him,
close to all who invoke Yahweh faithfully.

[19] Those who fear him need only to ask to be answered;
he hears their cries for help and saves them.
[20] Under his protection the pious are safe,
but Yahweh is destruction to the wicked.

[21] Yahweh's praise be ever in my mouth,
and let every creature bless his holy name
for ever and ever!

maker of heaven and earth, / and the sea, and all that these hold!
(*Psalm 146:6*)

Psalm 146

[1] Alleluia!

Praise Yahweh, my soul!
[2] I mean to praise Yahweh all my life,
I mean to sing to my God as long as I live.

[3] Do not put your trust in men in power,
or in any mortal man—he cannot save,
[4] he yields his breath and goes back to the earth he came from,
and on that day all his schemes perish.

[5] Happy the man who has the God of Jacob to help him,
whose hope is fixed on Yahweh his God,
[6] maker of heaven and earth,
and the sea, and all that these hold!

Yahweh, forever faithful,
[7] gives justice to those denied it,
gives food to the hungry,
gives liberty to prisoners.

[8a] Yahweh restores sight to the blind,
[8b] Yahweh straightens the bent,
[9a] Yahweh protects the stranger,
[9b] he keeps the orphan and widow.

[8c] Yahweh loves the virtuous,
[9c] and frustrates the wicked.
[10] Yahweh reigns for ever,
your God, Zion, from age to age.

Psalm 147

Alleluia!

1 Praise Yahweh—it is good to sing
  in honor of our God—sweet is his praise.

2 Yahweh, Restorer of Jerusalem!
  He brought back Israel's exiles,
3 healing their broken hearts,
  and binding up their wounds.

4 He decides the number of the stars
  and gives each of them a name;
5 our Lord is great, all-powerful,
  of infinite understanding.

6 Yahweh, who lifts up the humble,
  humbles the wicked to the ground.

7 Sing to Yahweh in gratitude,
  play the lyre for our God:

8 who covers the heavens with clouds,
  to provide the earth with rain,
  to produce fresh grass on the hillsides
  and the plants that are needed by man,
9 who gives their food to the cattle
  and to the young ravens when they cry.

10 The strength of the war horse means nothing to him,
  it is not infantry that interests him.
11 Yahweh is interested only in those who fear him,
  in those who rely on his love.

12 Praise Yahweh, Jerusalem,
  Zion, praise your God:

13 for strengthening the bars of your gates,
  for blessing your citizens,
14 for granting you peace on your frontiers,
  for feeding you on the finest wheat.

15 He gives an order;
  his word flashes to earth:
16 to spread snow like a blanket,
  to strew hoarfrost like ashes,

372

He decides the number of the stars / and gives each of them a name;
(*Psalm 147:4*)

17 to drop ice like breadcrumbs,
    and when the cold is unbearable,
18 he sends his word to bring the thaw
    and warm wind to melt the snow.

19 He reveals his word to Jacob,
    his statutes and rulings to Israel:
20 he never does this for other nations,
    he never reveals his rulings to them.

wild animals and farm animals, / snakes and birds,
(*Psalm 148:10*)

Psalm 148

[1] Alleluia!

Let heaven praise Yahweh:
praise him, heavenly heights,
[2] praise him, all his angels,
praise him, all his armies!

[3] Praise him, sun and moon,
praise him, shining stars,
[4] praise him, highest heavens,
and waters above the heavens!

[5] Let them all praise the name of Yahweh,
at whose command they were created;
[6] he has fixed them in their place for ever,
by an unalterable statute.

[7] Let earth praise Yahweh:
sea monsters and all the deeps,
[8] fire and hail, snow and mist,
gales that obey his decree,

[9] mountains and hills,
orchards and forests,
[10] wild animals and farm animals,
snakes and birds,

[11] all kings on earth and nations,
princes, all rulers in the world,
[12] young men and girls,
old people, and children too!
[13] Let them all praise the name of Yahweh,
for his name and no other is sublime,
transcending earth and heaven in majesty,
[14] raising the fortunes of his people,
to the praises of the devout,
of Israel, the people dear to him.

Alleluia! / Sing Yahweh a new song, / let the congregation of the faithful sing his praise!
(Psalm 149:1)

Psalm 149

[1] Alleluia!

Sing Yahweh a new song,
let the congregation of the faithful sing his praise!
[2] Let Israel rejoice in his maker,
and Zion's children exult in their King;
[3] let them dance in praise of his name,
playing to him on strings and drums!

[4] For Yahweh has been kind to his people,
conferring victory on us who are weak;
[5] the faithful exult in triumph,
prostrate before God they acclaim him
[6] with panegyrics on their lips,
and a two-edged sword in their hands

[7] to exact vengeance on the pagans,
to inflict punishment on the heathen,
[8] to shackle their kings with chains
and their nobles with fetters,
[9] to execute the preordained sentence.
Thus gloriously are the faithful rewarded!

praise him with clashing cymbals, / praise him with clanging cymbals!
(*Psalm 150:5*)

Psalm 150

FINAL CHORUS OF PRAISE

[1] Alleluia!

Praise God in his Temple on earth,
 praise him in his temple in heaven,
[2] praise him for his mighty achievements,
 praise him for his transcendent greatness!

[3] Praise him with blasts of the trumpet,
 praise him with lyre and harp,
[4] praise him with drums and dancing,
 praise him with strings and reeds,
[5] praise him with clashing cymbals,
 praise him with clanging cymbals!
[6] Let everything that breathes praise Yahweh!

Alleluia!